John Vigar has lived in Kent all his life and has a deep love of its people and places, especially the more off-beat examples. He is a freelance historian specialising in ecclesiastical architecture who lectures for the University of Kent, NADFAS and the National Trust. He leads study tours across Britain and is a Trustee of The Friends of Friendless Churches, a national charity. In addition to his voluntary associations with religious buildings he is Regional Field Officer across four counties for The Churches Conservation Trust, and the author of several books including *Kent Curiosities, Kent Churches* and *Kent: The County in Colour*. His hobbies include European travel and the history of the seaside resort.

KENT
BEDSIDE BOOK

*A Collection of Prose
and Poetry*

SELECTED AND INTRODUCED BY
JOHN E. VIGAR

THE DOVECOTE PRESS

First published in 2003 by The Dovecote Press Ltd
Stanbridge, Wimborne, Dorset BH21 4JD

ISBN 1 904349 21 8

© Introductions, John E. Vigar 2003

Typeset in Monotype Sabon
Printed and bound by The Baskerville Press Ltd.
Salisbury, Wiltshire

A CIP catalogue record for this book is available
from the British Library

1 3 5 7 9 8 6 4 2

CONTENTS

Introduction 6

Towns and Villages 9

By the Sea 38

Some Visitors 55

Accidents 65

Farming 79

The Big House 94

Church and Chapel 107

Kent at Work 117

Military Matters 124

People 140

Legends and Customs 157

Acknowledgements 159

INTRODUCTION

Many tens of thousands of words have been written about Kent. Poetry and prose, novel and guidebook – they represent the private and public views of people whose lives were as ordinary or extraordinary as our own. Whether writing for publication or intended for personal use they are always one person's view, and to anyone else who happens to read them it is almost impossible to get into the mind of the writer to determine exactly the point they wanted to make.

> This county being two-thirds of it bounded by sea and the river, the inhabitants thereof are kept more at home than they are in the inland counties. This confinement naturally produces intermarriages amongst themselves, and a relation once begun is kept alive and diffused from generation to generation. In humane and generous minds, which have always been the characteristic of this people, friendships and familiarities once commenced, are not easily dropped; and one needs not wonder that amongst such, affinities may sometimes be challenged where the lines may be worn out, or that the pleasantry of less considerate aliens should make a byword of such simplicity of manners.
> *The Revd Samuel Pegge quoted in* Archaeologia Cantiana, *1874*

Just as any writing is a personal view, so too is this selection. These extracts have made me laugh, cry, shudder with shock and – most importantly – think. I have endeavoured to present an anthology that sums up the character of what I believe to be one of the most diverse of English counties. As Richard Church wrote in *Kent* (1948): 'everything that has happened to the English people, has happened to the people of Kent first . . . Kentish folk have been the watchers at the door.'

In the eleventh century, the Men of Kent met William the Conqueror at Swanscombe, where a monument in the churchyard today commemorates the event, and there and then they were granted special rights and privileges that were not subsequently granted to other counties. It was this early recognition of a different status that gave Kent some of its independent character, which is summed up in these lines by Wordsworth:

To the Men of Kent

Vanguard of Liberty, ye men of Kent,
Ye children of a Soil that doth advance
Her haughty brow against the coast of France,
Now is the time to prove your hardiment!
To France be words of invitation sent!
They from their fields can see the countenance
Of your fierce war, may ken the glittering lance
And hear you shouting forth your brave intent.
Left single, in bold parley, ye, of yore,
Did from the Normans win a gallant wreath;
Confirmed the Charters that were yours before;-
No parleying now! In Britain is one breath;
We are all with you now from shore to shore:-
Ye men of Kent 'tis victory or death!

I hope you enjoy this selection of Kentish writing as much I have enjoyed compiling it. I have not changed any original spelling or punctuation, and hope that my notes will explain the questions the pieces raise. I sincerely hope that you will have as much fun reading them as I did.

I dedicate this collection to my mother, Alice Vigar (1914-2002) who first enthused to me about the county of my birth, and who knew and loved many of these works and the towns and villages about which they were written.

JOHN VIGAR, Aylesford, 2003

I · TOWNS AND VILLAGES

I love the small, hidden villages in the folds of the Downs, the windswept acres of the Romney Marshes and the market towns of the Weald. It is the architecture and the people that give these places their distinctive character and in the following selection I have tried to choose pieces that still – to some extent – reflect the character of the county today.

Canterbury

This Citie hath beene honoured with the presence and Coronations of King John and Queene Isabell his wife, with the marriages of King Henry the third, and of King Edward the first, and with the interments of Edward the Blacke Prince, King Henry the fourth, and of Queen Joan his wife: as Feversham is with the burials of King Stephen and Maud his Queene and wife. But as in glory so in adversity hath this Citie borne a part, being divers times afflicted by the Danes, but most especially in the dayes of King Ethelred, who in that revenge of their massacre, made havoc of all, and herein slew forty three thousand two hundred persons, the tenth besides reserved to live. Afterward it recovered breath and beautie by the liberalitie of Bishop Lanford: Charters and Priviledges by King Henry the Third; strength in Trench and Fortifications from King Richard the Second; and lastly, walls for her defence by Simon Sudbury Arch-bishop of that See: whose Graduation is placed for latitude 51.25 and parallelized for Longtitude 22.8 her sister Rochester differing not much in either degree.

John Speed, England, Wales and Scotland and Ireland Described, *1627*

Tonbridge Fair, 1810

O yes! O yes! O yes! This is to give notice
That on FRIDAY the 12th October – O ! aye, just so 'tis

TUNBRIDGE FAIR
Is to be held

At which all the good Gentlemen and pretty Ladies are invited
to meet together
And not to be at all afraid of any sort of weather.

THIS FAIR will certainly be usher'd in, in very grand Style;
Bells ringing – Drums beating – Colours flying – Cannons
roaring – *distant many a mile.*

But in the Afternoon, at 4 o'clock,
Young Ladies of good Character will be permitted to try their
Speed for a *Holland Smock.*
And *lusty lads*, from the Whip or Plough, may race it for a *New
Round Frock*

At Half-past Four
The *John's* will try their strength again, in running for a *Castor*,
And he that first gets to the Goal to be considered Master.

At Five
Three *grave Gentlemen* of 60 will add something to the Racket
And have a start to the Turnpike Gate for a *bran new Leathern
Jacket.*

At Half-Five

A *Neddy Race* for a *Gloucester Cheese* from the Chequer Sign-
Post

The winner of it is to be the one that comes in hindmost,
No Gentleman permitted to ride his own Ass.

At Six

To split your Sides with laughing, *two new Shoes*, worth two
Dollars

Will be *grinn'd for* by three Smilers thro'three Horse Collars.
With various other amusements.

The following Description of Persons are desir'd to keep away,
And not to shew their Faces until the second Day.

Light-finger'd Gentlemen, Ladies of *light Character*, the *Fighter*,
and the *Rover*,
As they will not be wanted before the Fair is over.

NB – Any Lady who takes more than 14 quarterns of Gin will
be considered a Disgrace to the Fair, and put into a Pigstye.

A Shortage of Tobacco in Gravesend

*Gravesend was once an important town for travellers, serving the
main London to Dover Road, as well as being the last main settlement
on the Thames downstream of London. A safe anchorage and port for
provisioning of ships, this early nineteenth century letter dwells
somewhat too much on the supply of 'pigtail' or tobacco for one of
the East Indiaman's crew:*

Warren Hastings, Est Indium, off Gravesend 24th March 1813

Dear Brother Tom – this cums hopein to find you in good health as it
leaves me safe ankored here yesterday at 4pm arter a pleasant voyage
tolerable short and few squalls; Dear Tom, hopes to find poor father
stout; am quite out of pigtail. Sights of pigtail at Gravesend, but
unfortinly not fit for dog to chor [chew]. Dear Tom – Captains boy
will bring you this, and put pigtail in his pocket when bort. Best in
London at the black boy 7 diles, where go, aks for best pigtail, pound
of pigtail will do, and am short of shirts. Dear Tom – as for shirts only
too too, whereof 1 is quite wored out, and tuther most, but don't forget

the pigtail as I ant had nere a quid to chor never sins Thursday. Dear Tom – as for the shirts, your size will do, only longer. I likes um long, get one at present, best at Tower Hill and be cheap, but be pertickler to go to 7 diles for best pigtail at the black boy, and Dear Tom, aks for pound of best pigtail, and let it be good. Captains boy likes pigtail so ty it up. Dear Tom, shall be up on Monday there or thereabouts. Not so particular for the shirt as the present can be washed, but don't forget the pigtail without fail. So am your loving brother T.P.

P.S. Don't forget pigtail.

Unknown source, quoted in 'Shrimps with Everything', John E Vigar, Kent Life 1985

Surnames in Gravesend and District

Camden, the great antiquary, declared, 'We have borrowed names from everything, both good and bad.' It is not surprising therefore, that English surnames should exhibit such an astonishing variety. ... I propose to give here a humorous arrangement of the surnames of some of the householders residing in Gravesend, Milton and Northfleet, at the present time (1889).

Let us, then, con the pages of 'Hall's Directory' and we shall find an extraordinary assemblage of individuals, who are stated to be Bigg and Tall, Little and Short, Littlemore and Shorter, Broad and Long, Low and Meen, Noble and Petty, Bond and Free, Rough and Wild, Savage and Wilder, Young and Nice, Still and Coy, Cross and Straight, Good and Wise, Sharp and Swift, Smart and Fitt, Forward and Earley, Neat and Askew, Dry and Bare, Strange and True, Rich and Gay, Bright and Best, Bonny, Blythe and Doughty. The good folk, as might be expected, have their share of Grief and Joy, Pain and Patience, Hope and Trust, Love and Bliss, ands Luck, Smiles and Pryde.

We find among them, too, 'all sorts and conditions of men.' Thus – a Surman, a Boorman, a Harman, a Sharman, a Chapman, a Tadman, a Bateman, a Tillman, a Couchman, a Fileman, a Steadman, a Foreman, a Cheeseman, a Packman, a Coleman, a Waterman, a Norman and a Bowman. Then we have a Goodman and a Badman, a Highman and a Lowman, a Newman and a Wiseman, a Youngman and a Smallman, a Freeman and a Brightman, a Redman and a Blackman, and (paradox of paradoxes!) a real live Deadman! In addition to these, there are four Masters, five Manns (the spelling here is rather *singular*), some nice Gals, a few Mailes and a Child or two. There are also two Friends, with another Frend who has lost an 'i' and a good old Soul in the neighbourhood.

We must not forget to mention, too, a bevy of eleven Darlings, three Deares, two loves, several Petts, a Truelove and a Fairey! But, marvel not, for is there not a Pettman (a young Swain), with two Rings and a Home ready! Anti-tobacconists please note! There are only three Smokers in the town and one of them is evidently Missing [*editor's note: Missing was a long-established Tobacconist in Gravesend*].

There is quite a troop of sons – Benson, Dickson, Williamson, Jackson, Jameson, Johnson, Ronaldson and Watson, Dadson, Beeson, Danielson, and Gibson, Tyson, and Mason. Yes, Gravesend is a 'sunny' neighbourhood. We have very few foreigners amongst us, there being just seven French, two Normans, a Celestial named Ching, six Blackmen, three Savages, four Jewisses, and some Cozens (probably from America). The others are 'real natives', composed principally of English and Welsh. We may mention, however, eighteen Scotts.

Our neighbourhood has a decidedly 'Upper-Ten'-dency, for have we not seventeen Kings (among whom are three Georges), two Princes, one Duke, two earls, one Noble, thirteen Knights, one Squire and some Gentry. These are attended by one Groom and seven Pages. There are two Courts, presided over by Messrs Chitty and Fray, assisted by six local Solomons. It is no wonder then that Law flourishes in our midst! We read of the Borough of Gravesend, but now we have two Burrows, and three Towns with four Wards. There is also a Thorpe. Although there are but one Street, eight Rows and two Roads in the place, we have not yet been free from Mudd and Myers! The number of Burgesses is astonishingly small, viz. eleven! While the local police force has been considerably reduced (there being just one Constable), the number of Berries has risen to three! [*editor's note: Mr Berry was at that time Superintendent at Gravesend Police Station*]. We must not forget to mention two trusty Beadles and a worthy Proctor! Calcraft is 'as busy as ever' in the town, and hint to those who kill Time. Church affairs are managed by a happy family of three Bishops (with two Creeds), five Deans, five Parsons, one Pope, two Abbots, three Priors, one Frier, one Monk, and four Nunns. The number of Pilgrims is extraordinarily small – namely two! While there is only one Christian! *O tempora! O mores!* Church accommodation is a very satisfactory item, there being no fewer than five Churches, with three Bells, and one Bellmore (NB – Only one Knell has been rung so far, the Sexton lives in Northfleet), four Kirks, two Chappells, and three Hermitages. It will be news to some to learn that Moody and Sankey are still amongst us!

We have amongst us, too, four Adams, who ought to be happy individuals for there are no less than ten Eves! There are besides Cain, Abel, Lott, Jacob, Levy, Sampson, Solomon, Samuel, David, Amos, Joel, Andrew, James, Bartholomew, Paul and a whole host of Matthews, Lukes and Stephens. We have a goodly list of trades and calling. Thus:- three Merchants, two Mercers, three Drapers, two Glovers, twenty-seven tailors, who have between them two Foremen and one Prentice. There are no cutters, strange to say, but probably this is through *shear* poverty.

Although there are no Schools, there are four Masters, with three Poynters and six Readers. Then we have a Goater, a Skinner, a Quilter, and a Stringer, and lastly, a noble army of sixty-five Smiths and six Wrights! Antiquaries will gladly note the presence of two Castles (containing three Chambers and four Wards), approached by a Drawbridge. There are adjacent, two Lodges, with eight Lofts, and a Whitehouse enclosed by three Walls. There are likewise, three fine old Postgates, and an interesting Bridge. Considering the size of the place, provisions are exceedingly scarce. What do we find? One Kitchingham, two Woodhams, a couple of Rolls, a Twist, some Whitebread, a little Honeycomb and some Bacon and Coffee.

In the matter of holidays, Gravesenders have a rare time of it, for are there not two Easters and a Christmas (with the inevitable Waites), besides one Holliday of two Weeks three Days! There is also a Loveday (February 14th, without doubt). The compass too is sadly out of gear, and need readjusting without delay. Just think! There are fifteen West, with two East and one North! Of colours, Brown appears to be the favoured hue, there being no fewer than twenty-five. There will, however, be a total of twenty-seven ere long, as there are two Browning! There are thirteen Whites to six Blacks, and two Blackmores. There are likewise eight Grays, three Lakes, one Pink, fourteen Greens and one Greener.

Extracted from The Kentish Notebook, *April 20th 1889*

Mud-rubbing and Mayors in Gravesend

Dear Henry, – We arrived here after a very pleasant voyage in one of the Calais steamers. Lobski, as usual, was, and is, quite at home. He really appears to be the flower of Gravesend. He spars with all the sailors who notice him, which are not a few – nods to the old women – halloes at the boys, and runs around with their hoops – knocks at the windows with his stick – hunts the fowls and pigs, because they run away with him – and admires the goats, because they are something new. As we walk on the beach he looks out for 'anoner great ship' – kisses the little girls, – thumps Mary – and torments me. The young ones in the road call him 'Cock Robin'. He is, indeed, what E.D. calls ' a tainted one'.

Upon first coming down I immediately commenced inquiries about the bathing and found some who talked of mud-rubbing. No one gave it such a character as Mrs. E-. I met with a lady on the beach, who told me she had brought a little boy of hers down last year to be mud-rubbed, but after a month's stay his legs were in no way improved – she then bathed him for a month, and the boy is a fine little fellow. I considered, as Lobski's legs really brought us here, it was best to bathe him at once, and accordingly paid 5s 3d for a month. Otherwise it is 1s each time. Since going in, which he took pretty well, considering the instantaneous plunge, he calls to me when he looks at the sea, 'There is my tub, Ma.' He was rather frightened, and thought he fell into the water, but not near so much, the guide says, as most children are. Harry is getting fatter every day, and very jealous of Bob when with me – but, out of doors, the little fellow glories in seeing Lobski run on before. They grow very fond of each other.

Monday will be a grand day here in choosing the Mayor, and at night a mock election takes place, with fireworks &c. and this day month the fair is held in the fields. The people here are anything but sociable, and 'keep themselves to themselves.' The sailors are most obliging, and are very communicative – they usually carry Bob over any dirty place or so for me – and, to tell the truth, I have almost changed my mind from a parson to a sailor. If you can, do come down on Sunday; but, by no means, empty-handed, or rather empty-pocketed – my cash is now very low, though I have been as saving as possible. I find no alteration in the price of provisions, except potatoes and milk – everything else I think is as in London. I should like some pens, paper and a book or two – for one, the Duchess D'Orleans' 'Court of Louis the XIV', I think it is – and anything, as poor Mrs L- says, 'wery amusing'; for the evenings are 'cursedly' – stop- it's your own word – and as I have said it, it may relieve a little on this evening's *ennui*. Whatever you bring you can put into the little portmanteau, which I shall find very useful when we return. Bob and Harry send you a kiss a-piece, and mine 'I will twist up in a piece of paper, and bring with me when I come to town.'

This is scribble – but Bob is asleep on my lap.

I am, my dear Harry,

Yours very affectionately

Hone's Table Book, 1828

Gravesend

In former days, on the 5th of November, Guy Fawkes generally proved a feast of revelry, in which all the devil-may-care instincts of the people seemed to be let loose, and it was scarcely safe for any peaceably disposed person to be at large. A favourite pastime of the mob was to lay hands on a boat in the river – a Norwegian pram for preference – fill it with tar, ignite it and draw it round the town, followed by a dense and excited crowd. In the narrower streets, such as High-street, this practice was attended with no little danger to adjacent property, and for protection the tradesmen took the precaution to put up their shutters to prevent anything untoward happening. It was not safe to leave any loose wood lying about, whether in enclosed yard or elsewhere, or it would be commandeered, and used for bonfires in various parts of the town, while lighted tar barrels were rolled about to the danger of life and limb. The Borough Police found these occasions very difficult to cope with, and it was a common occurrence on the following day for the Police Court to present the appearance of a hospital, so many of the police and civilians attending there wearing bandages round the head or other parts of the body in consequence of injuries sustained during the melee of the previous evening. By the efforts of Supt. White and his successor, Supt. Berrey, these rowdy demonstrations were greatly

ameliorated. Scenes of a similar description marked Mayor's Day –
the 9th of November – High-street and West-street being thronged
with excited citizens gathered to watch his Worship and retinue march
from the Town Hall to the banqueting chamber, which was then at the
New Falcon Hotel. We live in other conditions now, and occasions are
rare when the people let their passions run riot.

F.A. Mansfield, The History of Gravesend, *The Gravesend and Dartford
Reporter, 1922*

Sittingbourne

A notice recorded over a pub door in Sittingbourne in 1892.

Call frequently
Drink moderately
Pay honourably
Be good company
Part friendly
Go home quietly.

Sittingbourne

A Bulkin well knowne in divers places for his mad conceits, and his
couzenage, upon a time came into Kent to Sittingbourne; and in divers
Villages thereabout set up bills that all sorts of people, young and old,
that would come to Sittingbourne, on such a day, they should find a
man thereat would give a remedy for all kinds of diseases; and also
would tell them what would happen unto any of them in five or six
yeares after; and he would desire but two pence a piece of any of
them. Whereupon came people of all sorts and from all places; so that
he gathered of the people that came to the value of twenty pounds;
and he had provided a stage and set it up, and placed a chaire where
he would sit; and so, they being all come in, and every one set in order,
he comes to the gate and takes the money from them that gathered it,
and bids them looke that good rule be kept, and so they did; also hee
by and by sound the drumme, and then he would begin his orations.

He, when they were gone, with all haste, gets him to the backside, and there having his gelding, gets upon his backe, and away towards Rochester rides he, as fast as even he could gallop. Now they, thinking he had beene preparing of things in a readinesse, sounded the drumme. The Audience looked still when he would come, and staying one, two or three houres, nay more, thought sure they were cozened. Whereupon one of the Company seeing a paper in the chaire on the stage, tooke it, wherein was written,

> Now you have heard the sound of the drumme
> You may all depart like fools as you come.

Whereupon the men falling to cursing and swearing, the women to scolding, scratching and biting, were faine to depart like fools indeed.
Pasquil's Jests with the Merriments of Mother Bunch, *London, 1663*

A Romney Marsh Charter of 1252

This Charter of Henry III concerning the Ordinance of Romney Marsh show just how much power the Jurats of the area held, in that they were outside the county's jurisdiction. The maintenance of good sea defences was of course paramount, and Henry was determined that the people of this outpost should provide all that was required, and that his stretched finances should not be expected to cover it. Hence these privileges which had first been introduced over two hundred years earlier.

Henry by the Grace of God, King of England, Lord of Ireland, Duke of Normandy, and Count of Anjou. To all his bailiffs and faithful subjects, to whom these present letters shall come, Greeting. Because, by four and twenty lawful men of Romney Marsh, time out of mind hereunto chosen and sworn, distresses ought to be made upon all those which have lands and tenements in the said Marsh, to repair the Walls and Watergages of the same Marsh against the danger of the sea, and also upon all those which are bound and charged for the reparation of the said Walls and Watergages: we have granted to the same four and twenty, that for the safety of the said Marsh, they cause those distresses to be done, so that they may be made equal according to the portions greater and lesser, which men have in the same Marsh, and according to that to which some are bound and charged. And therefore we will and grant, that no Sheriff of ours in Kent, or any of his bailiffs, do in any wise intermeddle touching those distresses made by consideration of the aforesaid four and twenty Jurats to avoid the same danger. For whosoever shall bring complaint unto us, in consideration of those distresses, we will cause justice to be done unto him in our court, and that justice we reserve specially to ourself, or at our special commandment.

In witness whereof, these letters we have caused to be made patent. Witness myself at St Edmunds the second day of September in the six and thirtieth year of our reign.

Close Roll, 36 Henry III, m.4

In Romney Marsh

As I went down to Dymchurch Wall,
I heard the south sing o'er the land;
I saw the yellow sunlight fall
On knolls where Norman churches stand.

And ringing shrilly, taut and lithe,
Within the wind a core of sound,
The wire from Romney Town to Hythe
Alone its airy journey wound.

A veil of purple vapour flowed
And trailed its fringe along the straits;
The upper air like sapphire glowed;
And roses filled Heaven's central gates.

Masts in the offing wagged their tops;
The swinging waves pealed on the shore;
The saffron beach all diamond drops
And beads of surge, prolonged the roar.

As I came up from Dymchurch Wall,
I saw above the Down's low crest

The crimson brands of sunset fall
Flicker and fade from out the west.

Night sank: like flakes of silver fire
The stars in one great shower came down;
Shrill blew the wind; and shrill the wire
Ran out from Hythe to Romney Town.

The darkly shining salt sea drops
Streamed as the waves clashed on the shore;
The beach, with all its organ stops,
Pealing again, prolonged the war.

John Davidson, 1890

Toasts in Hayes village school

Mr Till, Rector of Hayes for nearly fifty years, was a man much beloved by his parishioners, and his memory is still cherished with deep respect and affection. To an amiable disposition he added a considerable share of pleasantry and dry humour. The following impromptu toasts which he gave at the village school-feasts, in which he much delighted, are worth preserving:

'May our school be the friend of the Church and the Crown:
May it often break up;- May it never break down'

and

'May virtue and learning still thrive in our School
And our duty to God and the King be our rule.
May we keep to this rule to the end of our days,
And always remember we learnt it in Hayes.'

and finally

'May our School be kept up by the wise and discerning
And always be famed for plum-pudding and learning.'

George Clinch, Antiquarian Jottings, *1889*

Dickens describes Rochester

*In one of Dickens' best pieces of descriptive writing, his home town
of Rochester is thinly disguised. Its single street, its courtyards and its
medieval walls jumbled against later buildings are still there today. So
too is the Nuns' House, now the Charles Dickens Centre.*

An ancient city, Cloisterham, and no meet dwelling-place for anyone
with hankerings after the noisy world. A monotonous, silent city,
deriving an earthy flavour throughout from its Cathedral crypt, and
so abounding in vestiges of monastic graves, that the Cloisterham
children grow small salad in the dust of abbots and abbesses, and
make dirt-pies of nuns and friars; while every ploughman in its
outlying fields renders to once puissant lord treasurers, archbishops,
bishops and suchlike, the attention which the ogre in the story-book
desired to render to his unbidden visitor, and grinds their bones to
make his bread.

A drowsy city, Cloisterham, whose inhabitants seem to suppose,
with an inconsistency more strange than rare, that all its changes lie
behind it, and that there are no more to come. A queer moral to derive
from antiquity, yet older than any traceable antiquity. So silent are the
streets of Cloisterham (though prone to echo on the smallest
provocation), that of a summer day the sun-blinds of its shops scarce
dare to flap in the south wind; while the sun-browned tramps, who
pass along and stare, quicken their limp a little, that they may the
sooner get beyond the confines of its oppressive respectability. This is
a feat not difficult of achievement, seeing the streets of Cloisterham
city are little more than one narrow street by which you get into it,
and get out of it: the rest being mostly disappointing yards with
pumps in them and no thoroughfare – exception made of the
Cathedral Close, and a paved Quaker settlement, in colour and
general confirmation very like a Quakeress's bonnet, up in a shady
corner.

In a word, a city of another and a bygone time is Cloisterham, with
its hoarse cathedral bell, its hoarse rooks hovering about the cathedral
tower, its hoarser and less distinct rooks in the stalls far beneath.
Fragments of old wall, saint's chapel, chapter-house, convent and
monastery, have got incongruously or obstructively built into many of

its houses and gardens, much as kindred jumbled notions have become incorporated into many of its citizens' minds. All things in it are of the past. Even its single pawnbroker takes in no pledges, nor has he for a long time, but offers vainly an unredeemed stock for sale, of which the costlier articles are dim and pale old watches apparently in a slow perspiration, tarnished sugar-tongs with ineffectual legs, and odd volumes of dismal books. The most abundant and the most agreeable evidences of progressing life in Cloisterham are the evidences of vegetable life in many gardens; even its drooping and despondent little theatre has its poor strip of garden, receiving the foul- fiend, when he ducks from its stage into the infernal regions, among scarlet-beans or oyster-shells, according to the season of the year.

In the midst of Cloisterham stands the Nuns' House: a venerable brick edifice, whose present appellation is doubtless derived from the legend of its conventual uses. On the trim gate enclosing its old courtyard is a resplendent brass plate flashing forth the legend: 'Seminary for Young Ladies. Miss Twinkleton'. The house-front is so old and worn, and the brass plate is so shining and staring, that the general result has reminded imaginative strangers of a battered old beau with a large modern eye-glass stuck in his blind eye.

Charles Dickens, The Mystery of Edwin Drood, *1870*

A Smuggler's Epitaph

Romney Marsh was well known for its smuggling activities and in Lydd Churchyard is this inscription to George Walker, a smuggler shot whilst escaping from the court room:

'Let it be known that I am clay
A bace man took my life away
Yet freely do I him forgive
And hope in Heaven we both shall live,
Wife and children I've left behind
And to the Lord I them resign
I hope He will their steps attend
And guide them to a happy end.'

A Headcorn Childhood

I was born in the 1920s in Headcorn, a sleepy little village in the Weald of Kent, number three in a family of four children. Father was a poultry farmer in the days when the birds ran about free as the wind – no loathsome factory farms or battery cages then. As well as the flocks of chickens we kept turkeys, geese and bantams, also our much-loved pony, lots of cats and a dog and numerous pet rabbits. Our house stood in eight acres of land which included two orchards and two lawns – one large enough to play tennis or croquet, or even a slightly restricted game of cricket! Remembering my two son's childhood in a small town garden with just two cats I often think how very lucky we were – but childlike we took it all for granted and often grumbled about the jobs we had to do to help out on the farm .

For a long time we had no gas, electricity or running water. Every morning Father would fetch our drinking water from the 'big house' about half a mile away, but the water for washing and all other purposes was brought up in buckets from one of our four ponds. Our privy (or toilet) was in the garden, a pretty little hut covered in honeysuckle and pink rambler roses, very picturesque in summer, but on dark winter nights with snow and ice and wind whistling it was hell! We used to 'bottle it' until the last moment and then put on coats and scarves and make a dash for it! Saturday was the worst day as Mother always gave us a dose of syrup of figs on Friday nights – I need say no more.

West Kent within Living Memory, *Countryside Books, 1995.*

Newenden

The village of Newenden is still very much a frontier town, as described 450 years ago by Kent's first county historian, William Lambarde.

The situation of Newendene is such, as it may likely enough take its name, either of the deepe and bottome (as I have conjectured) or of the Hil and high ground, as Leland supposed. For it standeth in the valley, and yet clymeth the hill: so that the termination of the name may be Dene, or Dune, of the valley, or of the hill, indifferently. Howbeit, I would easily yeeld to Leland in this matter (the rather, because the common people of that quarter speake much of a faire Towne, that sometime stood upon the hill). Saving that both many places thereabouts are upon like reason termed Denes, and that John Bale (who hath seene an auncient hystorie of the house itself) calleth it plainly Newendene.

It is a frontier, and Marchier Towne of this Shyre, by reason that it lieth upon the River that divideth Kent and Sussex in sunder there, which water Leland affirmeth to be the same that our auncient Chronicles call Lymene, though now of the common sort it is knowen by the name of Rother only.

William Lambarde, *A Perambulation of Kent*, 1576

Taking the waters in Tunbridge Wells

That indefatigable traveller, Celia Fiennes, visited Tunbridge Wells in 1697, nearly a century after the discovery of the Spa.

I being in Kent this year shall insert something of Tunbridge the waters I have dranke many years with great advantage, they are from the Steele and Iron mines, very quick springs especially one well, there are two with large basons of stone fixt in the earth with several holes in the bottom by which the springs bubble up and fill it, so as it always runns over notwithstanding the quantity dipp'd up in a morning – which is the usual tyme the company comes – and the nearer they drink it to the spring the better, it being a spirituous water that is ready to evaporate if carry'd any way, as has been try'd by weighing the water by the Well and carrying them but to the middle of the Walks it has lost of the weight, and much more the end of the whole Walke; notwithstanding, many has it brought to their lodgings a mile or two off and drink them in their beds, nay some have them brought to London which is near 40 miles; they have the bottles filled and corked in the well under the water and so seale down the corks which they say preserves it.

They have made the Wells very commodious by the many good buildings all about it and 2 or 3 mile round, which are Lodgings for the Company that drinke the waters, and they have increased their buildings so much that makes them very cheape; all people buy their own provision at the Market which is just by the Wells and furnish'd with great plenty of all sorts flesh fowle and fish, and in great plenty is brought from Rhye and Deale etc., this being the road to London, so all the season the water is drank they stop here which makes it very cheape, as also the Country people come with all their back yard and barne door affords, to supply them with, and their gardens and orchards which makes the markets well stored and provision cheape, which the Gentry takes as a diversion while drinking the waters to go and buy their dinners it being every day's market and runns the whole length of the Walke, which is between high trees on the market side for shade and secured with a row of buildings on the right side which are shopps full of all sorts of toys, silver, china, milliners, and all sorts of curious wooden ware, which this place is noted for the delicate neate and thin ware of wood both white and Lignum vitae wood; besides which there are two large Coffee houses for Tea Chocolate etc., and two roomes for the Lottery and Hazard board; these are all built with an arch or pent house beyond the shops some of which are supported by pillars like a peasa, which is paved with brick and stone for the drye walking of the Company in raine, else they walke with out which is a clay and sand mixed together – they have been intending to make it gravel which would be much better – all those conveniency's are added by the Companyes contributions every year, what has been and so what will be.

There is at the lower end of the Walke, which is a broad space before you come to the walls of the Wells, where is a large sun dial set up on severall steps of stone; thence you go straight along to a Chapple which has been built by the severall collections of the Company every year; it's a pretty place and cost a great deal of money and every year there is a contribution for the maintenance of a minister; there are severall buildings just about the Well where are severall apothecary's shops there is also a roome for the Post house; the Post comes every day and returns every day all the while the season of drinking the waters is, from London and to it, except Mondayes none comes down from London, so on Satturdayes non goes up to London; you pay a penny Extraordinary for being brought from Tunbridge town which is 4 mile distance, that being a post town, you likewise have the conveniency of Coaches every day from London for 8 shillings apiece dureing the whole season and Carriers twice a week.

The Journeys of Celia Fiennes, *The Cresset Press*, 1947

And from a different perspective . . . there follows a late seventeenth century satire on the people who came to Tunbridge Wells both to drink the water from the Chalybeate Spring and to be part of fashionable Society for 'the season'. Tunbridge was an unfashionable spa that was barely regulated – in comparison to Bath – even at this early date, before the arrival of Beau Nash and was very much seen as a poor man's resort. The author makes it clear what he thought of some of the visitors, and how much or little he hopes they will benefit from their stay.

Of a Place like to *Tunbridge* I never heard yet,
So fruitfull of Poets, so barren of Witt;
Yet the subject is vast, here is *Shute* and *Throgmorton,*
Here are *Colby's* false Dice, *Cornish Wroth* and Beau *Norton,*
Of its Bullies and Knaves fam'd *Westminster's* bereft,
And in *London's* great Citty not a Cuckcold is left.
Here's of every Profession, Degree, Sex and Age,
From a handsome young Dutchess to a Pert Quaker's Maid.
Here are some have a deep, and some no design,
Some enquire after News, but more after Coyn.
Some Raffle, and some at the *Oak* crowd to win,
While the Lady *Ann Poppham's* chief Game's In and In.
Now in my Poetical Rapture I'le sweare
The Unpowdered Dark Consul is Charmingly faire,
Tho' his Barley-fac'd Mistress does his Judgement betray,
In choosing a Wanton so foolish and gay.
And now I have begun, I will not omit
Sir H. Fur's honesty, Courage and Wit.
Hem, Hem! Go on, if you stumble at this
At Court your affairs will all go amiss.
Jack Meers, of him pray have patience; *Jack Meers*
Is always as wise as at first Sight he appears.
Dick Syms is a hero, *Sir Ed.* a Phisitian,

And his Lady, I'm told, is a deep Polititian.
So much for Encomium; now I'll make true verse on
The Whiffing Lord *Hawley's* insignificant Person;
But the Creature, himself can best ridicule,
I need not expose him, for hee's his own foole.
His fleering Gay Partner declares against Marriage,
But what shee'l admit you may see by her Carryage.
Now, if I may add one Satyricall Lash,
I think Sir *Dudley Cullum* below Sir *Ja. Ash*.
And now all the rest I think I will spare,
Who if I would describe I could sooner declare
How many pray'd for the Assassination
Since Political spite disgraces our Nation.
However, next post I will make some amends,
And (like a true poet) fall on my best friends,
Beau *Letton* and *Howard*, *Sharp*, *Skelton* and *Fitz-James*,
The *Ingrams*, and *Fairbanks* shall all be my game.
Nor will I forget that dear Mistress *Cox*,
Whose name not improperly Rhimes to red Locks;
Nor *Cleaveland*, nor *Goodman*, each Sexe's disgrace,
Shall not in this mourant Paper have place.
But by *Delphick Apollo*, I'll Rhime day and night
To do the admired Lady *Ranelagh* right,
To describe all her features and wonderful Charmes,
And the brisk Cuckold-maker that's blest in her Armes.
If the Coxcombs are curious to know who I am,
My self I'le describe, tho' I'le not tell my Name.
I have *Sharp's* Reason, and Sir *J. Her's* face,
I smell like Proud *Howard* and dress like his Grace,
I dance like Judge *Treby*, like *Mordant* I drink,
I grin like *Dr Sherlock*: like *Cesar* I think,
Like *D'urfey* I scribble and live in dull ease.
Of a Place like to Tunbridge, *1692, British Library, Harleain Ms. 6947, fol. 215*

And in the nineteenth century . . .

The tone and character of the architecture of this place, in which such
vast opportunities existed in exhibiting it in perfection, is nevertheless,

and in general, rather pleasing than striking. It may be called the 'Modern English,' which by attempting to follow the severer rules of the Grecian, disdaining the Roman, except to mistake it, and not knowing the Lombard style, or being itself too much akin to the Tudor and Vandalic taste, has fallen into a jumble that can only be designated by the national denomination I have bestowed upon it. This style is like nothing else. It has prevailed for the last twenty years in all places where much building has been going on, whether in the capital or in the chief cities of counties, and at watering-places. You see it triumphant in the Regent's Park, Park-terrace, and Hyde-Park-gardens. You meet with it at Brighton, on the extreme East Cliff, and on the King's-road. You cannot mistake it at Cheltenham. It is getting on pretty smartly at Leamington; and we find it here also, especially on the Calverley Estate. A richer, more unique, more magnificent, or extensive locality for the display of sound, yet handsome domestic architecture, than this very domain, no man of taste or judgement could possibly have desired. Yet not one truly striking edifice has been erected upon it; and the hotel, the houses on the terrace and parade, with here and there a detached villa within the park, are the only specimens one can single out as being superior in style to the generality of the 'Modern English.'

Augustus Granville, Spas of England and Principal Sea Bathing Places, *Adams and Dart*, 1971

Tunbridge Wells

Here Richard Cobb describes his visits to Tunbridge Wells Library just before the Second World War.

There was a regular clientele of poorly dressed male and female readers – though two of them could hardly qualify for that rather grand title, for I never caught them in the act of reading, they just stared sightlessly ahead of them – the former sitting in their dirty macs, wheezing, expectorating, picking their noses or their teeth, or both, and talking to themselves in a regular low murmur. The women were quieter, though there was one, very hunched and tiny, who made high-pitched whistling sucking noises, the origins of which could be traced to oblong paper packages, like tiny bolsters, in bright yellow, and bearing letters in bright red, and that contained evil-looking black coils of liquorice. I quite often stopped there, to take a look at the papers which we did not get at home, and to read the *Connoisseur* and the *Studio*, which, apart from myself, did not seem to be very much in demand, though the liquorice lady would linger for hours over the *Field* and the *Sporting Life*. It was no use trying to get hold of *The Daily Telegraph*, which was regularly monopolized by one of the men – I suppose he made a grab for it as soon as the place opened in the morning – who would not relinquish it till he had finished the crossword, and this would take him much of the day.

Very occasionally I would look in in the morning, before my eleven o'clock drink in the pub that was in a small building that must have at one time been the stables of the Calverley Hotel and that was now mostly used by the waiters and domestic staff of the place when they were off-duty, and by a wonderfully talkative lady in a changeless and somewhat greasy black toque called *Maud*. Maud seemed as permanent a fixture of the single-roomed pub as were the 'readers' of the room up on the first floor. But, more often, I would stop off there in the early afternoon, on my way to the top end of the town. Very rarely, I would look in in the evening, on my way back. I think most of them – the number varied from ten to a dozen – must have stayed there throughout the opening hours. In the afternoons, there would be empty, greasy-looking paper bags in front of their places on the three long tables, the remains, I suppose, of whatever they had brought with them for lunch. Life upstairs in the Reading Room had a reassuring immobility about it, very much in contrast to the bustle and noise of the ground floor, with people coming and going, women and small children, I suppose from the unknown areas behind the old Town Hall, handing in books and taking out new ones. Although the Reading Room stocked *Modern Boy*, *Beano* and the *Childrens Newspaper*, and whatever weeklies or monthlies addressed themselves to schoolgirls, I never saw any children, whether in the uniforms of one of the local schools, or dressed more casually, in the room upstairs. Perhaps, at some previous time, one or two had ventured up there and had been frozen out by the angry stares of the regulars, who certainly did not look as if they had had any children of their own or would have had much time for children in a general sense. Even I, in my twenties, could feel the unspoken disapproval of their glances; it was pretty clear that I was much too young to gain proper admittance, as a full-paid-up-member, to a wonderfully poor and shabby version of a very exclusive club. Or it may have been that I was too well-dressed and was seen as letting down the high standards of frayed shabbiness that was expected of anyone seen regularly up there. But habit wears down most such unwritten and unspoken rules, and , in the course of time, I could feel myself being granted a rather grudging acceptance despite my clothes and my youthful appearance. After a time, two of the regular male readers, both senior members, judging from their seats – one next to the window, the other with his back to the spluttering fire – even gave me a look of recognition: a very slight concession to a timid sociability. Of course, in such a place, there could be no question of anyone actually *greeting* anyone else, and though, as I have said, there was a regular, even, low buzz of conversation, it was entirely self-addressed. Now and then individual words and exclamations would be distinguished: *Well, I never, Blow me down*!, *Who would have thought it*!, *Utterly disgraceful*! (a literary intrusion, possibly), and, once, in a very upper class voice, *By Jove!* indicating, like the *utterly*, that the club seemed to offer a pretty wide social range. It even occurred to me that the *By Jove!* reader might have been one of the six local hermits. The nearest thing to a conventional conversational exchange was when the liquorice lady caused a shocked temporary silence among the steadily low-pitched droners by saying quite distinctly, and in very broad Kent: *Shut up!* This was clearly an appalling breach of decorum; but it was the only time that I heard anything of the kind. The series of low-pitched drones soon picked up again like the steady hum of machinery. The incident had presumably been forgotten and forgiven. There was a notice, in black letters on a washable white – not *very* white – background, over the glass-fronted bookcase, marked with the word SILENCE. I took this to mean – and so presumably did my seniors – that this signified not talking to anyone else. The steady low drone was really part of the silence, like the popping hum of a gas-fire or the smooth murmur of a generator.

Richard Cobb, *Something to Hold Onto*, John Murray, 1988

Maidstone, 1760

Here Virgins, dress'd so neat are seen,
They're neat without, because they're pure within.
Here *Chloe* trips it with a decent pride
With all the *Graces* duly waiting at her side.
Here *Clara*, too, – who wou'd not *Clara* wish to kiss?
Her voice is Rapture, and her Presence Bliss.
A few old Maids, 'tis true, do here reside,
Who have rejected all the Honours of a Bride;
Howe'er, they're useful Harbingers of *News*,
Glean'd from late visits and their *Sunday*-Pews!
So calm and quiet is each Street and Lane,
That envy, discord, here is sought in vain;
Coaches on Coaches rattle thro' the street,
Only at balls, when Beaux and Beauties meet,
Such happy Walks are here in sylvan shade,
Design'd for faithful Swain and his Virtuous Maid!
Aspiring Hops, and fields of plenteous Corn,
Each opening Landscape everywhere adorn,
Here rural Innocence, Industrious toil,
Makes families innumerable smile:
One stated Labour is their Steady gain,
Each labour'd Day does its own Cares maintain.

George Austen, A few extempore verses on the Old Maids of Maidstone, 1760

Higham

Gad's Hill was later to become the home of Charles Dickens, but the area was already famous for its literary connections.

'Gad's Hill,' immortalised by Shakspeare, as the scene of the exploits of Sir John Falstaff, is 26 miles from London; and in the year 1676, a gentleman was robbed about 4 o'clock in the morning, by a man named Nicks, who, to prevent detection (as he afterwards confessed), proceeded to Gravesend, where he was detained nearly three hours, for want of a boat to convey him across to Essex, for Chelmsford; he then proceeded to Braintree, Bocking and Wethersford; over the Downs to Cambridge, keeping the cross-roads to Godmanchester and

Huntingdon, by Fenny and Stratford, where he baited his horse, and slept about half an hour. He then rode full speed to York, (198 miles N. by West of London) where he arrived in the afternoon. Here he changed his dress, and mixed with a company in the bowling green, and soon selected out the Mayor of that City, of whom he enquired the hour of the day; who pulled out his watch and told him it wanted a quarter to eight. Some time after, Mr Nicks was prosecuted for the robbery, and the whole merit of the case turned upon this single point. The person who had been robbed, *swore to the man;* but Nicks produced the Mayor of York, who proved his being at the Bowling Green on the day in question. The jury, therefore, acquitted him, on the supposition, that it was *impossible* for him to be the man, and also to be in York on the same day.

Mockett's Journal, *1789*

Lympne

Lympne is a small village built on a sandstone ridge overlooking the Romney Marshes. It is dominated by an impressive church and castle which was formerly the home of the Archdeacons of Canterbury. At the base of the escarpment runs the Royal Military Canal, built in the early nineteenth century to counter a French invasion, and the ruins of the Roman Stutfall Castle. The author H.G. Wells lived at Sandgate, a few miles to the east of Lympne and his novel, Kipps, *about a young man who strives to improve his situation in life is predominantly set in this part of the county. Here the young Kipps takes his ladyfriend on an expedition.*

Every one who stays in Folkestone goes sooner or later to Lympne. The castle became a farmhouse, and the farmhouse, itself now ripe and venerable, wears the walls of the castle as a little man wears a big man's coat. The kindliest of farm ladies entertains a perpetual stream of visitors, and shows you her vast mangle and her big kitchen, and takes you out upon the sunniest little terrace-garden in all the world, and you look down the sheep-dotted slopes, to where, beside the canal and under the trees, the crumbled memories of Rome sleep for ever. One climbs the Keep, up a tortuous spiral of stone, worn now to the pitch of perforation, and there one is lifted to the centre of far more than a hemisphere of view. Away below one's feet, almost at the bottom of the hill, the Marsh begins and spreads and spreads in a mighty crescent that sweeps about the sea, the Marsh dotted with the church towers of forgotten mediaeval towns, and breaking at last into the low blue hills by Winchelsea and Hastings; east hangs France between the sea and sky; and round the north, bounding the wide perspectives of farms and houses and woods, the Downs, with their hangers and chalk-pits, sustain the passing shadows of the sailing clouds.

And here it was, high out of the world of every day, and in the presence of spacious beauty, that Kipps and Helen found themselves agreeably alone. All six, it had seemed, had been coming for the Keep; but Mrs Walshingham had hesitated at the horrid little stairs, and then suddenly felt faint, and so she and the freckled girl had remained below, walking up and down in the shadow of the house; and Coote remembered they were all out of cigarettes, and had taken off young Walshingham into the village. There had been shouting to explain between ground and parapet, and then Helen and Kipps turned again to the view and commended it, and fell silent.

Helen sat fearlessly in an embrasure, and Kipps stood beside her.

'I've always been fond of scenery, ' Kipps repeated, after an interval.

Then he went off at a tangent. 'D'you reely think that was right what Coote was saying?'

She looked interrogation.

'About my name.'

'Being C-U-Y-P-S? I have my doubts. I thought at first – What makes Mr Coote add an 'S' to Cuyp?'

'I dunno, ' said Kipps, foiled. 'I was jest thinking'.....

She shot one wary glance at him, and then turned her eyes to the sea.

Kipps was out for a space. He had intended to lead from this question to the general question of surnames and change of names; it had seemed a light and witty way of saying something he had in mind, and suddenly he perceived that this was an unutterably vulgar and silly project. The hitch about the 'S' had saved him. He regarded her profile for a moment, framed in weather-beaten stone, and backed by the blue elements.

He dropped the question of his name out of existence, and spoke again of the view. 'When I see scenery – and things that – that are beautiful, it makes me feel -'

She looked at him suddenly, and saw him fumbling for his words.

'Silly like,' he said.

She took him in with her glance, the old look of proprietorship it was, touched with a certain warmth. She spoke in a voice as unambiguous as her eyes. 'You needn't,' she said, 'You know, Mr Kipps, you hold yourself too cheap.'

Her eyes and words smote him with amazement. He stared at her like a man who awakens. She looked down.

'You mean -'he said; and then, 'Don't you hold me cheap?'

She glanced up again and shook her head.

'But – for instance – you don't think of me – as an equal like.'

'Why not?'

'Oo! But, reely-'

His heart beat very fast.

'If I thought -'he said; and then, 'You know so much.'

'That's nothing,' she said.

Then, for a long time, as it seemed to them, both kept silence – a silence that said and accomplished many things.

H.G. Wells, Kipps, Everyman, 1993

Some Kentish Rhymes

Long, lazy Lewisham, little Lee,
Dirty Deptford and Greenwich free.
Sutton for mutton, Kirby for beef,
South Darenth for gingerbread, and Dartford for a thief
[These villages are along the Darent Valley.]

He that would not live long
Let him live in Murston, Teynham or Tong.
[This refers to then unhealthy north Kent marshes.]

He that rides in the Hundred of Hoo
Besides pilfering seamen, will have dirt enoo'.
[The Hoo Peninsula was remote and untamed.]

He that would go to a church miswent
Let him go to Cuxton in Kent.
[The chancel and nave of Cuxton church are built out of alignment, a common medieval problem of determining due east from the position of the sunrise, which changes depending on the time of year.]

Proud Town Malling, poor people
They built a church onto their steeple.
[The oldest part of West Malling church is its Norman tower].

When England wrings
The island sings
[A reference to the dry climate of the Isle of Thanet.]

He was born down Ryarsh sandpits
[Then a common phrase to describe an illegitimate baby.]

They were married in Finglesham Church
[There is no church at Finglesham, implying that the couple are living in sin.]

Earl Godwin and his court are hungry
[A saying of the Deal fisherman when a storm was brewing, referring to the possible loss of their ships on the Goodwin Sands.]

Smuggling on Wrotham Heath

Whilst we associate smuggling with the Kent coast and Romney Marsh in particular, many Kent villages were on established distribution routes, enabling goods to be carried cross country from their point of landing to their major market – London. One of the best known areas was Wrotham as this extract shows:

Free traders or Smugglers of the eighteenth and early nineteenth century were not persons to be despised by their neighbours and are referred to here as those gentlemen who avoided the Duty imposed by the Law. There is a clear connection between the 'Free Traders' of Wrotham and what was known as the Wood Street business in the

City of London. Wrotham was the home of some of these men, who made this village their head centre, for it was the last halt on the road from Deal, Romney and Sandwich en route for London. Immediately above Wrotham village on the downs is 'Old Terry's Lodge', formerly a mansion and estate, now a hamlet by a few cottages known as 'Old Terry's'. Close by was the site of the chief Beacons where the old Traders (or smugglers) had their telegraph station, a large scaffold-like erection of timber with great plank arms, nearly as large as the arms of a windmill; these were pulled up and down, to the right or left, 2 or 3 at a time in various positions, similar to the semaphore signals on railways nowadays.

This telegraph line was in the line of vision of another at Shooters Hill and at Boxley Hill. Those Free Traders in Wood Street, London receivers of tobacco, laces and spirits (known as 'Old Weeds', 'Old Rope Yarn' and 'Old Dusty') were fairly safe but had to pay smartly at times when things were traced to them. News of the presence of Excise or Preventive men was telegraphed to the men on the Downs by different formations of cattle; for caution ' don't be seen', three cows or horses would be tethered together in various ways. At night time the low house showed a light at one end or both ends or in three places. Some fifty horses could be mustered with neighbours 'Old Gates', 'Old Catcher' and others at Ightham, Wrotham Heath and Crouch, sometimes two hundred for a big run. The regular meeting place was where Platt Grange now stands; at that time the land was common or waste land. The men involved were not wholly dependant upon horses, since they also used dog-carts; a splendid pair of strong dogs which had made the journey many times and knew the route perfectly – one of the dogs whose home was at Wrotham Heath would run with one whose home was the Marsh, and vice versa, a method of travel so swift that not infrequently the old stage-coaches were overtaken by these 'canine carriers' and the quickest mode of dispatching news to the 'front'.

Landing on the coast took place according to signs given on 'Flashers', a sort of pistol without a barrel; it had a flintlock and a pan to contain a quarter thimble full of powder, a good stock of which was always carried in powder-horns, approximately 4 inches long, to fit into a waistcoat. On the return inland from the coast the gang broke up for their various 'hides' to dispose of their stuff; a suitable one was

Wrotham Heath, a good position for watching the telegraph system, with nothing to break the view to Hurst Woods, Crouch and along Ightham Common and Caesars Camps. In fact every smuggler seemed to have permission to poach for rabbits anywhere; they deterred the poachers and ladies of some houses encouraged their hiding so as to avail themselves of purchasing something without Duty. Even the squire was not too anxious to know how tobacco, silk handkerchiefs, etc. came into his possession.

The kitchen folk were all in favour of these men who brought tea, silk and other things in his pack, under his coat-tails or a petticoat with a large pocket or bladder containing the finest Brandy or Hollands. On one occasion some 20 horses with a swag consisting of Kegs (holding 4 gallons each) and bales of silk weighing 20lbs each were tracked down by the Preventive men who traced the stuff to an old quarry at Platt, stored in a shed known as 'Thatched Down', a shed with thatched sides. Extra men, however, were needed from the Barracks at Maidstone; meanwhile the smugglers working at the back of the lodge made a hole large enough to pass small packages out, which were quickly carried up into 'Potter's Hole' and there placed in another 'Hide'

John Terry, Reminiscences of an old Free Trader, *1888*

Se'noak Fair: An extemporal Burlesque

This type of song was very popular in the late eighteenth and early nineteenth centuries. Whilst the names of real people were replaced with descriptions of their characteristics, they were so finely disguised that anyone at the time would have recognised who was being talked about. Miss Dorothy Fuzz was not a pseudonym, but the name of a famous singer of the day. The other names appear to be fictitious. The tale ends with the narrator having a less than satisfactory experience that he felt should have been the crowning glory of his day at the Fair!

In numbers most humble, I'll carol the FAIR:
There was *Simon* and *Dolly* – and who was not there?
Was e'er such a meeting so fair to the eye,
Not a cloud or a vapour obscured the sky;

In the dress of gay summer, *Autumnus* was seen,
The landscapes so smiling! the foliage so green!
O'er the stiles and o'er gates, thro' each meadow and lawn,
With many a laugh and with many a yawn,
Comes *Roger*, and *Rachel*, and *Johnny* and *Joan*,
In round frocks so new, and so flower'd a gown,
Now fearless of masters' or mistresses' frown,
St *Michael* is past, and the time is their own.
Blest freedom, thy power pervades high and low,
What breast but is warm'd with thy ravishing glow!
I love care parental, and filial duty,
As much as my eye is delighted with beauty:
With pleasure I see then old *Timothy Hazy*,
With *Nelly* his daughter, as fresh as a daisy,
An old dapple grey, come jogging along,
And as they com' mix with the hustling throng,
They stop and attend to a wonderful song;
For music has charms, and amidst all this buzz,
Who is not delighted with *Dorothy Fuzz*?

Along with Miss *Camblet*, Miss *Pinck*, and Miss *Pimple*,
I spied a fair maid with an innocent dimple,
Not array'd in her ribbons, her gauzes and gimp,
Nor servility's child, nor of fashion an imp;
Not beauteous, tho' fair, but there beam'd from her face
The rays of good-nature, and elegant grace;
Her stature not tall, unconfin'd in her air,
So I call'd her the Goddess of *Sevenoaks Fair*,
And begg'd her permission, before it was dark,
To leave the sweet *Fair*, and to traverse the park.
To *Knowle* then I went, and impatient to see
(*Old worn-out magnificence*), made my congee
To a half finish'd thing, who seem'd proud of a key;
Uninstructed herself, I learn'd nought from her blab,
So tipt her a fee, and took leave of Miss *Crab*;
Took leave of the park, and the building antique,
And quitted the *Fair* with some kind of dislike.
The Kentish Muse, The Canterbury Journal, *November 18–25 1783*

2 · BY THE SEA

Think of Kent and you think of her coastline. Brash Margate, gateway Dover, unspoiled Broadstairs and pescatorial Whitstable. Yet each is unique, having developed to suit the different requirements of successive decades. Kent's coastal resorts were amongst the first to be developed, offering something for everyone. Or almost everyone!

Herne Bay

A sort of fatality seems to hang over Herne Bay, a spot which poses, one would think, natural attractions of its own sufficient to have insured for it a career of uninterrupted prosperity. Here is a fine beach, admirably adapted for bathing; a sheltered bay, open, nevertheless, on the south to the fresh breezes of the German Ocean, beautifully wooded, and charmingly diversified inland country, and, with the exception of Brighton, the nearest point of the sea coast to the great metropolis, from which it is distant, as the crow flies, something short of sixty miles. Just as Herne Bay, however, has managed to secure its direct line of railway, it is compelled to forgo the advantages and attractions of its pier, which is in a sufficiently advanced stage of decay to be permanently closed to the public. Still with a railway, which brings visitors down from London in little more than a couple of hours, Herne Bay can very well manage to put up with the loss of its steamboat communication with the metropolis, which was never to be entirely depended upon. It is mainly as a promenade for visitors that the pier will be missed.

It would be affectation to pretend that our first impressions of Herne Bay are not somewhat melancholy in character. The place presents a too vivid picture of decay in action to be entirely pleasant. You encounter tumble-down carcases of houses at the very entrance to the town; ... The pier presents a melancholy spectacle; the gates are closed and barricaded, and a notice intimates that the public are forbidden to walk on it owing to its dangerous condition. The notice is certainly superfluous, for, staring us in the face, is one of the toll-houses with its roof off, and portions of its walls in a state of ruin. The very flooring of the pier is full of great gaps, from the decay of its timbers, and the side railings are fast rotting away... Even the Clock Tower, which will be noticed in the centre of the Parade, the liberal gift of Mrs Thwaites, the widow of some wealthy city grocer, and most kind patron of Herne Bay, has begun to exhibit unmistakable symptoms of decay. The swimming bath, too, at the western end of the Parade is now a mere dry cave, from the openings in which branches of trees may actually be seen protruding.

The Parade itself extends along the edge of the beach from west to east for upwards of a mile, and forms, as may be imagined, an admirable, and now that the pier is enclosed, a much-frequented Promenade. Facing it there are one or two good hotels, and numerous stylish-looking houses, with others of a less pretentious character, most of which have pretty looking gardens in front of them.

It was not, however, until 1830 that any particular efforts were made to bring Herne Bay into notice. In that year a splendid scheme was set on foot. A new town was projected; the streets and squares of which were actually laid out, and the foundations dug, as a walk through the vacant spaces at the back of the houses on the Parade will testify. Through operations being commenced on too large a scale the grand scheme was speedily doomed to come to grief, and the projectors had great difficulties in getting even the range of houses fronting the sea completed.

Herne Bay, in spite of the disappointments it has been doomed to suffer, keeps up its pluck in a measure, and does what it can to attract visitors. Fancy its having a couple of assembly-rooms - one forming part of the establishment known as St George's Baths; the other the Brunswick Assembly Rooms . . . It also has its hall, where the Literary and Scientific Institution meets, and where amateur dramatic performances are now and then given by a corps of amateurs.

There is thoroughly good bathing to be had at Herne Bay - as good, indeed, as at any point of the coast. Besides several bathing establishments, there are three sets of machines - one at the west, and two at the east end of the Parade. At Herne Bay one meets with none of that boisterous vivacity which distinguishes the public bathing at Margate, and which appears to call for constant and rigid supervision on the part of the corporation of the town - on the contrary, everything is precise and proper as it should be, and paterfamilias may stroll about the beach without running the risk of being shocked at anything he witnesses.

All About Margate and Herne Bay, *1864*

Ramsgate

Rest on these cliffs, and breathe the bracing air;
Around you spreads a Kentish picture fair;
March blithely on the smooth, far-stretching sands,
Survey the Goodwins, where brave hearts and hands
Go forth to save. Or on the noble pier
As the sou'wester hurtles fiercely near,
Taste health as round you dash the show'rs of spray:
Each blast blows languor of the brain away.

J. Pratt, The Weekly Dispatch, *late 19th century*

Dover

The Piers which form the Haven, or large Basin, are costly and great Works . . .Several Acts have passed to repair and restore the same . . . Dover is one of the Cinque Ports, and ...here most of the Business of these ports in general is done, and the Courts are kept . . . The Packets for France go from here, in time of Peace, as also those for Ostend, with the Mails for Flanders; and all those ships which carry Freights from New York to Holland and from Virginia to Holland, come generally hither, and unlade their Goods, enter them with the Custom-house Officers, pay the Duties, then enter them again by Certificate, re-load them, and draw back the Duty by Debenture, and so they go away for Holland.

By a Gentleman, A Tour thro' the Whole Island of Great Britain, *1762*

The Warden of the Cinque Ports

The Duke of Wellington was one of the most famous Lord Wardens of the Cinque Ports. His official residence, Walmer Castle, was a favourite home, and the room in which he died may still be visited. These lines, reflecting the nation's shock at the death of such a prominent figure, are by Longfellow.

A mist was driving down the British Channel,
The day was just begun,
And through the window-panes, on floor and panel,
Streamed the red autumn sun.

It glanced on flowing flag and rippling pennon,
And the white walls of ships:
And from the frowning rampart, the black cannon
Hailed it with feverish lips.

Sandwich and Romney, Hastings, Hythe and Dover,
Were all alert that day,
To see the French war-steamers speeding over,
When the fog cleared away.

Sudden and silent, and like couchant lions,
Their cannon through the night,
Holding their breath, had watched, in grim defiance,
The sea-coast opposite.

And now they roared at drum-beat from their stations
On every citadel;
Each answering each, with morning salutations,
That all was well.

And down the coast, all taking up the burden,
Replied the distant forts,
As if to summon from his sleep the Warden
And Lord of the Cinque Ports.

Him shall no sunshine from the fields of azure
No drum-beat from the wall
No morning gun from the black fort's embrasure
Awaken with its call!

No more, surveying with an eye impartial
The long line of the coast,
Shall the gaunt figure of the old Field-Marshall
Be seen upon his post!

For, in the night, unseen, a single warrior,
In sombre harness mailed,
Dreaded of man, and surnamed the Destroyer
The rampart wall has scaled.

He passed into the chamber of the sleeper,
The dark and silent room,
And as he entered, darker grew, and deeper,
The silence and the gloom.

He did not pause to parley or dissemble,
But smote the Warden hoar;
Ah! what a blow! that made all England tremble
And groan from shore to shore.

Meanwhile, without, the surly cannon waited,
The sun rose bright o'erhead;
Nothing in Nature's aspect intimated
That a great man was dead.

G. *Saintsbury*, Poems of Longfellow, *(1906)*

Deal

Deal is a seaport without an harbour; but the Downs between the
shore and the Goodwin Sands affording a secure road for ships, the
town is usually crowded with a succession of visitors and persons

engaged in maritime affairs; passengers also being usually landed here, letters brought on shore, provisions taken in, and vessels, both outward and homeward bound, commonly waiting for orders and instructions....The custom house, naval storehouse, and hospital, afford convincing proofs of its flourishing condition and increasing opulence. The pilots stationed here are esteemed remarkably skilful, both old and active; and the assistance afforded by them to vessels in distress, whether belonging to the royal navy or private traders, entitles them to be marked amongst the most useful and effective classes of British sailors. The appearance of the Downs, when enlivened by the arrival of a large fleet, is extremely interesting, and exhibits a noble proof of the naval strength and commercial importance of the country.

As the inhabitants of Deal may be considered almost amphibious, and the attention of those who visit the coast will be principally directed to its fine beach and the shipping, the buildings of the town, and the distribution of the streets, must not be too fastidiously criticized. If they appear dirty and narrow in those parts to which the greatest traffic occasions the greatest resort, some allowance must be made for the low and level shore on which the houses were originally erected, and for the meanness of the buildings themselves, constructed at a period when, in all probability, there was but little expectation that Deal would ever arrive at its present degree of opulence and importance.

Deal affords a complete contrast to Sandwich. On visiting the latter, a stranger, as he wanders solitary through the town, in which "the pavement dreads the turf's encroaching green", and scarcely a human being is visible even at noon-day, will be induced to ask, Where are the inhabitants? But as soon as he arrives at Deal, he is surrounded by so great a throng as to obstruct his passage along the streets, and he is tempted to exclaim, Where can such a multitude find habitations?

L. *Fussell,* A Journey Round the Coast of Kent, *1818*

Many improvements are going on at Deal and Walmer where lodgings have at this early period of the season become scarce . . . From the high price of land in its immediate vicinity (some has sold at £200 per acre) and the preparations that are making for building, we have no doubt it will ere long rank high in the estimation of the public.

Maidstone Journal and Kentish Advertiser, *June 1825*

Deal's need for Improvement

I am not a native of your town, but I have been in it for long enough
to observe that it is half a century behind most watering-places. While
its near neighbours, Dover and Ramsgate, can boast of their artificial
harbours, and Margate of its piers, and also of the numerous lodging
houses, from their elegant and commodious terraces . . . down to the
humble cottage where the shopman or artisan may enjoy his annual
holiday. To such attractions as these Deal has no pretence . . .with the
exception of three Gingerbread castles and an irregular range of
antiquated buildings, Deal sea frontage is as innocent of the crime of
improvement as when Julius Caesar landed nineteen centuries ago.
Now, Sir, these things need not be . . . Why not form a company for
the erection of an iron pier . . . you would soon find it necessary to
alter and increase the number of lodging houses; trade in general
would flourish and be the making of the town.

Anonymous correspondent, The Deal, Walmer and Sandwich Telegram, *1859*

Shakespeare Cliff

Dover's Shakespeare Cliff, and the recently reclaimed land at its foot,
Samphire Hoe, both take their names from this scene in 'King Lear':

[Enter *Gloucester* and *Edgar*]

Gloucester	When shall we come to the top of that same hill?
Edgar	You climb up it now: look, how we labour.
Gloucester	Methinks the ground is even.
Edgar	Horrible steep. Hark, do you hear the sea?
Gloucester	No, truly.

Edgar.   Come on, Sir: here's the place: stand still. How fearful
    And dizzy 'tis, to cast one's eyes so low!
    The crows and choughs that wing the midway air
    Show scarce so gross as beetles: half way down
    Hangs one that gathers Samphire, dreadful trade!
    Methinks he seems no bigger than his head:
    And fishermen, that walk upon the beach
    Appear like mice: and yond' tall anchoring bark,

Diminish'd to her cock; her cock, a buoy
Almost too small for sight; the murmuring surge
That on the unnumber'd idle pebbles chafes
Cannot be heard so high. I'll look no more:
Lest my brain turn, and the deficient sight
Topple down headlong.

William Shakespeare, *King Lear,* Act IV, Scene VI

Folkestone

I am inclined to think that it is impossible to be ill at Folkestone. The
air is magical, and the spirit of the place is benevolent. The holiday-
makers' part of the town, lying behind the Leas, is inoffensive enough,
while the shops are distinctive. That general good humour which is a
characteristic of the people of Kent is heightened at Folkestone into a
positive kindness. .. Folkestone is an entity, as complete as that of a
charming woman. It has grace and beauty.

Richard Church, Kent, Robert Hale, *1948*

Folkestone's Petition to Charles I

*In the seventeenth century, Folkestone had reached a nadir. Trade was
being lost to Dover, cross channel traffic was decreasing and the
town's economic problems were not being helped by coastal erosion.*

To the King's most excellent Majestie
The humble peticion of the Maior, Jurates, & Co'ialtie
Of the towne of ffolkstone and others charitably
Disposed and well affected to the place.
   Humbly sheweth that the Town of ffolkstone in the Countie
of Kent, hath heretofore flourished by meanes of fishing and trade
by sea, and hath furnished very hable Pilots and Mariners for the
Kingdome's service, and from time to time hath contributed great
Summes of money towards the setting forth of shipps; but is now
of late fallen into great decay and the inhabitants become very
Poore; by meanes the sea (working some alteracions upon the

Coast) hath of late fetched in, and carried awaie their ancient
Stade or station, where their vessells were used to be layd up in
Safety. So that they are altogether deprived of the meanes to
secure their barques, and consequently of convenienecy of trade
and fishing; and the sea likewise by washing, beating, and under-
mining the Cliffs hath encroached and woon soe much upon the
land that is approached within seventie paces of the Church,
which standes upon the said Cliff, soe undermined, and threatened
in short to winne the same (as heretofore yt hath fetched in
two other churches there) if speedy course be not taken to stoppe
the breach upon the shoare and defend the violence of the
Sea.

Your Peticioners therefore humbly crave that your
Majestie will be gratiously pleased to give licence by roiall graunt,
under your Majestie's great seale unto your said Peticioners for
building a Peare and harbour there at theire owne charges, with
like rights dutyes benefits and privileges as other places of harbour
have obteyned and doe enjoy from the roiall bountie of your
Majestie or your Majestie's predecessors. And in regard of their
povertie & that they have undertaken the charge of soe great a
worke, chiefly out of charitie of others well affected to the common
good, They further humbly praie that your Majestie will give order
by yor princely command that your said roaill graunt in that
behalf may be passed by ymediate warrant and without fees. Your
Majestie shall thereby cause that the Church shall bee secured, the
fishing and trade restored, the number of Mariners increased, your
Majestie's customes advanced, and a multitude of poore people
by their lawful endeavours relieved. And your petitioners shall
continually praie for your Majestie's long and happie raigne.

His Majestie for soe good & charitable a worke is gratiously
pleased to graunt the Petitioners this their suit as in the Petic'on
is desired. And his Majestie's Attorney Generall is to prepare a
graunt accordingly ready for His Majestie's roiall signature.
Theo:Suffolke

Quoted in M. Woodward, The Past and Present of the Parish Church of
Folkestone, *1892*

Frank Muir on holiday in Ramsgate

Good holidays stick in the memory and I have complete recall of one trip which turned out to be quite perfect. I was travelling alone and I packed fussily with care and precision, emptying out my case and beginning again until all my holiday things lay in neat, unruffled order.

When the day of departure came at last I bade farewell to my loved ones, picked up my heavy case and off I went. I had three days of good food, late nights, sing-songs, games and laughter and then returned home with happy memories.

I was aged six. I had spent the holiday at the Derby Arms Hotel, Ramsgate, Kent, the pub in which I was born, which was 100 yards down the road and kept by my granny.

A pub is an excellent place for a holiday when you are young and impressionable. The Derby Arms was excitingly crowded and noisy on Friday and Saturday nights with a penny-in-the-slot mechanical piano plonking away and a great deal of loud singing of sad songs; the favourites in the public bar were 'Way Down Upon the Swanee River' and 'There's a Long, Long Trail A-Winding', both sung slowly and sorrowfully with deep feeling. The favourite tipples were pints of mild and bitter (a mixture of the two draught beers), stout, and, for ladies in funds, port and lemon (a tot of tawny port topped up with fizzy lemonade).

My brother Chas and I were not supposed to go into the bar, but we could see in and we would sneak in whenever possible to be nearer the action.

At weekends the bars were packed with sailors from the boarding houses up the hill and miners from Chislet colliery and Irish navvies working on the new railway line; there must have been some outbreaks of rowdyism and violent behaviour but I cannot remember seeing or hearing any in the years when I grew up there. Perhaps because the working man had just survived a war and was not taking his pleasure in a fight but a bit of fun; the local pub was his equivalent of radio, TV, theatre, music hall and bingo - and his wife was usually with him. Another factor was that our granny had a glittering eye like the ancient mariner and a very powerful, indeed awesome personality when provoked.

The Derby Arms Hotel was well positioned for a pub, being on the outskirts of Ramsgate on the main road to Margate. Just along the road, McAlpine's built a huge brick viaduct to carry the express trains from London over the Margate road to the new Ramsgate station and my brother Chas and I watched it being built.

Better still, we watched when the viaduct was tested by a convoy of six enormous railway engines which, like a family of elephants, huffed and puffed backwards and forwards across the viaduct, hissing steam and blowing their whistles triumphantly. For two small, boys - very heaven.

On the far side of the road to the pub stood a grey, granite horse trough, much appreciated in summertime by the huge shire-horses in the brewer's dray when the pub's beer was delivered. It was a long pull from the town. In the granite on the front of the trough a message was chiselled saying that it had been donated by a local resident, the creator of The Scarlet Pimpernel, Baroness Orczy.

To my delight, a beer delivery took place on the Saturday morning of my perfect holiday. The dray was backed up to the front of the pub and two enormous draymen, not so much born as drawn by Beryl Cooke, jumped down and hooked back the huge trapdoors in the pavement. A special squat and very strong ladder was then lowered into the cellar; this ladder did not have normal wooden rungs but curved iron bars, which allowed the heavy wooden barrels to be safely slid down.

In the cellar where I crouched, overexcited and probably half drunk from the heavy fumes of beer which permanently hung in the cellar air, all was cobwebs, bent lead piping running from the barrels to holes in the ceiling, wooden spigots and mallets, and lots of dust.

The massive draymen rolled a barrel off their dray and slid it down the ladder where it thudded onto a sandbag at the bottom. Granny's cellar man Fred then manhandled the barrel up a little ramp onto its rack. Four full barrels were delivered and then the four empties were pulled up the ladder by Spanish windlass (a rope looped round the barrel's tummy with one of its ends fastened to the top of the ladder and the other hauled upon).

During my holiday the weather was warm and sunny and I was taken for long walks. Facing the Derby Arms was an old sunken country lane which was my favourite walk. It led through cornfields gashed with scarlet poppies (Don't lie down and fall asleep near the poppies or you'll be drugged by the opium and never wake up'), past St. Lawrence College, Ramsgate's public school, eventually coming out on the main road near the Brown Jug pub, Dumpton Park, nearly at Broadstairs. The lane had the ancient and melodious name of Hollicondane.

At the side of the Derby Arms was a road leading uphill to where a new railway station was being built with the help of my father, who had a little wooden hut all to himself and was putting up a mile stretch of iron railings alongside the station's approach road. The hilly road up which my father walked to work every morning went past what was, in the last century, a rough and quite dangerous conglomeration of lowly boarding houses, slop shops and grocers called the Blue Mountains - a nickname almost certainly bestowed by Australian seamen from Sydney, which has a range of hills behind the city known as the Blue Mountains.

Until recently most pubs were called hotels and years ago they probably did provide accommodation of a modest 'commercial gentleman' nature. The Derby Arms Hotel could well have been built for that kind of trade.

Upstairs on the first floor there was a penny-in-the-slot loo for ladies, and my brother Chas and I, on our way up to bed or bath, grew used to making our way up the stairs alongside cheery ladies breathing out fumes of Mackeson's milk stout and hauling themselves up by the banisters towards comfort.

One afternoon I crept into the ladies' loo - utterly forbidden territory - to find out what mysteries lurked there, and managed to lock myself in. As the pub was closed and my granny was resting, I had to cry myself hoarse before rescue arrived.

On the floor above were some small chill bedrooms where commercial gentlemen might once have been thriftily accommodated. At the age of six I thought there were about fifty bedrooms up there, but as I grew older the number shrank to more realistic estimates, until one day I counted them and found that there were three bedrooms, plus a couple of tinier rooms which had a bath and a loo,

In these bathrooms, above each enamelled iron bath crouched a Ewart's 'Victor' geyser, a gas-fired engine of copper and brass which had to be operated with caution and bravery.

The lighting operation was an act of faith. It required a good supply of matches and an iron nerve. An arm had to be swung out from the belly of the machine and the pilot light on the end of it lit. It was reluctant to go 'plop' and produce its tiny blue flame and often had to be warmed up first, which might take half a box of Union Jack matches, though there was some compensation in that the matchbox had a joke on the back. (Sample joke on the back of a Union Jack matchbox; 'Mummy, mummy! Johnny's swallowed a sixpence!' Mother: 'That's all right, its his dinner money.')

Then the lit pilot light had to be swung back into the stomach of the engine. This action opened up all the main gas jets which hissed threateningly for a moment and then, touched by the pilot flame, exploded with a great 'WHOOSH!' If you swung the arm in too slowly or - and I've never understood the scientific reason for this - if you swung the arm in too swiftly there could be an explosion which charred the eyebrows. Ever since those days I have never been happy putting a match to gas.

After a few minutes of gestation the geyser's nozzle began to deliver a thin trickle of steamy water at a temperature of about 2,000 degrees centigrade.

A huge room which must once have been the function room of the 'hotel' took up most of the first floor. It had a faintly Far Eastern smell to it, probably from the Chinese bits and pieces of furniture with which the room was stuffed; brass gong-like tables on fretworked teak folding legs; huge black lacquered screens with mother-of-pearl cockatoos flying across them; faded little framed watercolours of junks on the Yellow River and distant mountains capped with snow. The oriental smell probably lasted because the windows seemed to be kept tightly shut even in mid-summer. During the ten years or so when I more or less lived in the Derby Arms I had the feeling that I was the only person who ever went into that room.

Frank Muir, A Kentish Lad, *Bantam Press, 1997*

Rosherville

When Gravesend was a thriving holiday resort, cashing in on its proximity to London, numerous attractions grew up in the vicinity. The most popular attraction were the Rosherville Gardens, overlooking the River Thames upstream of Gravesend.

The Gardens of Rosherville; sweet, safe, shady and salubrious thing between the Thames and the Tiber.

If in London's streets you grill,
all is cool in Rosherville.

By a river, or a rill,
you may dream at Rosherville.

Tower and Temple, vale and hill
all are found at Rosherville.

If a woman's voice you thrill,
all are *belles* at Rosherville.

Archery here shows your skill
cupid shoots at Rosherville.

If you'd vote your troubles *nil*,
pass the vote at Rosherville.

Here one never sees a bill
smiles are cash at Rosherville

Life's moss-roses here distil
all are sweets at Rosherville.

If you're well, or if you're ill,
come full speed to Rosherville.
The Revd G Croly, *Lines on Rosherville*, c.1850

Margate

This strangely moving poem contrasts the bustle of Margate before the war with its appearance in 1940 at the height of the Battle of Britain.

From out the Queen's Highcliffe for weeks at a stretch
I watched how the mower evaded the vetch,

So that over the putting-course rashes were seen
Of pink and of yellow among the burnt green.

How restful to putt, when the strains of a band
Announced a *thé dansant* was on at the Grand,
While over the privet, comminglingly clear,
I heard lesser 'Co-Optimists' down by the pier.

How lightly municipal, meltingly tarr'd,
Were the walks through the Lawns by the Queen's Promenade
As soft over Cliftonville languished the light
Down Harold Road, Norfolk Road, into the night.

Oh! Then what a pleasure to see the ground floor
With tables for two laid as tables for four,
And bottles of sauce and Kia-Ora and squash
Awaiting their owners who'd gone up to wash -

Who had gone up to wash the ozone from their skins
The sand from their legs and the Rock from their chins,
To prepare for an evening of dancing and cards
And forget the sea-breeze on the dry promenades.

From third floor and fourth floor the children looked down
Upon ribbons of light in the salt-scented town;
And drowning the trams roared the sound of the sea
As it washed in the shingle the scraps of their tea.

Beside the Queen's Highcliffe now rank grows the vetch,
Now dark is the terrace, a storm-battered stretch;
And I think, as the fairy-lit sights I recall,
It is those we are fighting for, foremost of all.

John Betjeman, 'Margate 1940' in Collected Poems, *John Murray, 1958*

How long can we stay?

Sir.- There are complaints on all sides as to the shortness of the Margate Season compared with other places; but does the town do anything to induce the visitors to prolong their stay? On the contrary, the 1st October means the day for a great change, for whatever the weather may be and the number of visitors still remaining, the Extension band leaves, places of amusement close, certain shopstalls shut and some outdoor seats are removed. The cheap fast trains are taken off, and practically everything says 'the season is over; you may go'. Surely if a little were done for the continued comfort of visitors, Margate like other places, might have an autumn season, and even some winter visitors. The meteorological observations show that Margate is essentially a healthy winter resort. Why then should not the town exert itself to keep the people instead of practically inducing them to leave?

Yours truly

A LADY VISITOR

Keble's Gazette, 9th October 1886

Margate, 1906

There is only one Margate in the world. It is like no other place, and no other place is like it. And yet with its strongly distinctive character it constantly suggests to the travelled visitor certain distinguished features from other popular health and pleasure resorts.

Walk from end to end of its humanly fascinating and Nature favoured 'front' and you are reminded as you roam of Eastbourne, Hove, Blackpool, Folkestone, Yarmouth, Scarborough, Bournemouth and Dover. There is a point just beyond the Jetty where for a moment you may even recall Southend. You pass it and in a few seconds you are in a region so refined, a haven of such old-world seclusion by the sea, that you are not in the least surprised to discover that the building opposite you is a Home of Rest for the Clergy.

At one end of a glorious green stretch of cliff land you are in Merry Margate that throbs through the day with an honest joy of life; at the other end you are in Magnificent Margate, where impassive Millionaires lounge in dignified attitudes on flower-framed terraces that carry your thoughts to Cannes...You may stroll in one five minutes to Hove in the height of the fashionable season, and in another five minutes to Blackpool in a Bank Holiday.

G.R. Sims, Margate, *PTO August 11th 1906*

A Reward for Catching Smugglers

TWO HUNDRED POUNDS REWARD
Whitehall, 6th April 1830

Whereas it has been humbly represented to the King,
that about two o'clock in the morning of Wednesday.
the 31st ultimo, a large party of armed Smugglers feloniously
assembled on the Sea Shore, near Dymchurch, in the county
of Kent, and were aiding and assisting in the illegal landing,
running, and carrying away of unaccustomed Goods; and that
in opposing this felonious act, and in seizing part of the said
Goods, Lieutenant Gustavus Spicker Baker, and Martin
Donovan, seamen, both of His Majesty's ship "Talavera",
were attacked, violently beaten with clubs, and severely
bruised.

His Majesty, for the better discovering the persons who
have been guilty of this felony, is hereby pleased to promise
his most gracious Pardon to any one or more persons
so assembled (except those who actually committed violence
on the said Lieutenant and Seaman on this occasion) who
shall discover his accomplices, so that they may be
apprehended and brought to justice.

ROBERT PEEL

And the Lords Commissioners of the Admiralty hereby
offer a Reward of Two Hundred Pounds, to be paid to, or
distributed amongst, any person or persons (except, as
aforesaid) who shall give information to Captain Pigot, of
the "Talavera", or to any of the Officers of the said ship, as
shall lead to the discovery, apprehension, and conviction, of
the said offenders: such Reward to be payable by Mr
CHARLES JONES, the Solicitor of the Admiralty and Navy, on
the conviction of the said offenders, or any of them.
John Wilson Croker

3 · SOME VISITORS

When one travels through an unfamiliar area, one notices things that the locals don't. If they are at all out of the ordinary, the inclination is to write them down. Similarly when someone extraordinary visits an area it is the locals who put pen to paper. With a county as criss-crossed by roads as Kent is, it is unsurprising to find such a wealth of travel writing.

Rochester in 1635

From hence I am to passe to Rochester, and in the midway, I fear'd no robbing although I pass'd that woody, and high old, robbing hill on which I alighted, and tooke a sweet and delightful prospect of that faire streame, with her pleasant meades she glides through, and fertile downes of either county, a long and broad way. My way was very pleasant and faire to Rochester, which I found situated in a sweet and pleasant valley, having gliding by it a delightful and brave River, that runs through the heart of this county from the Towne of Bridges and passing by her on 2 partts; over which to enter her, I mounted over a faire, stately, long and strong Frestone Bridge, of 11 goodly arches, with strong battlements and iron railes, all along on both sides, the which for its length, and without buildings on it, is not much inferior to that unparallel'd Londons. This was built at the very great coste and charge of a noble Knight and coped with iron by a right reverend Archbishop. The water noyseth, ebbeth and floweth at every tide, according to the breadth of the stream, as that other doth. Close upon the banke of that sweete stream, and not farre from the bridge, stands an old and ruinated castle, of which there is yet soe much remaining as a man may adventure an ascent of 140 staires up to the top thereof, without any great danger. The moddell of this building sheweth strength and antiquity; the yarde is about 2 acres wall'd about, and hath on it 10 towers, whereof there are 6 still standing, the other 4 being quite ruinated, and those that yet stand are much decay'd; it is also in trench'd in with a ditch, into which they wold let in the flowing of the tide at pleasure and drowne it, which was an additonall strength thereunto. As I found this Citty little and sweet, so I found her chiefe and best structures correspondent to her smallnesse, which was neat and hansome, and neither great nor sumptuous.

And first I'le begin with her chiefe seat the Cathedrall, which was consecrated in Hen. I time; and though the same bee but small and plaine, yet it is very lightsome and pleasant; her quire is neatly adorn'd with many small pillars of marble; her organs, though small, yet are they rich and neat; her quiristers, though but few, yet orderly and decent; her Pallace and Deanery though both little, yet are they both hansome and lively. Her monuments are but few, yet they are very ancient. First, 2 Bishops in blew marble, in their pontificall postures lye flanking either side of the High Alter, so ancient as without name or inscription; yet one of them is suppos'd to be Bp Gundulphus who built a great part of the Castle, and that Tower yet standing there. He was appointed by Wm the Conqueror principall Surveyor of that great worke, the building of that stronge and famous Tower of London. He also new built this Church more faire than itt was before, and increas'd her revenues much. The monuments of Bp Merton, Lord Chancellor to Henry the 3rd and Founder of Merton Colledge in Oxford. Two old monuments, one in freestone, the other in blew marble. The monument of one Mr Stritton, who had been 9 times Commaunder of the silver ore there. Sir Alexander Temple's monument with his lady; and some few other of churchmen and citizens, of later years, which I will here omit, and divers others also of antiquity, so dismembered, defac'd and abus'd as I was forc'd to leave them to some better discovery than I was able to render of them; as also the venerable shrine of St William.

In the Pallace, I view'd that which is not usuall in such a place, the Armory, which was taken away from a Lord not farre remote from that city, in a little island thereby, by the Ld Bishop of this diocesse, upon a speciall command from our late Soveraigne for some speciall reasons and there kept; and when prayers were done, I march'd from the Cathedrall into the city again, which I found govern'd by a Mayor, with his mace and 12 alderman. Betweene this Citty and Chattam, in that sweete streame where his Majesties Navy securely rides, I view'd 10 stately, goodly, faire ships newly equipped and trimm'd, well victuall'd and mann'd, ready to be sent to the rest of the Fleet; but just at that instant of my being there, there came a command from His Majestie for their stay and discharge, which made those press'd soldiers and sailors swarm, thereabouts like bees and busy as gnats, and (as it was much afear'd) would have beene much more busy, if strict and speciall care had not beene speedily taken over them, which might very well hasten travellers away the sooner, not to run the hazzard of being benighted. Therefore away from the Kings Head, in the chiefe street there, I posted to the next poste Towne.

A Short Survey of the western counties of England by a Lieutenant, a Captaine and an Ancient of the Military Company of Norwich. *British Library, Lansd. MS. 213*

[Our travellers left Gravesend. The 'robbing hill' is Gad's Hill, later the home of Charles Dickens. The 'town of bridges' is, of course, Tonbridge. Rochester bridge was partially founded by Sir Robert Knowles (a 'knight'). The 'commaunder of the silver ore' is the Mayor, and the armour was confiscated from Lord Forster on the Isle of Sheppey. The next posting town from Rochester was Sittingbourne.]

Beware - Highwaymen!

About eight at night, four ladies and a gentleman, going down Shooters Hill in their carriage, were stopped by three foot-pads, armed; one of them stood at the horses' head with a blunderbuss, while the others got into the carriage and demanded their money, which they took, amounting to about £40.00

Kentish Gazette, *April 18th 1795*

A Foreign Visitor's View

In the eighteenth century many young gentlemen travelled to the continent. This 'Grand Tour' allowed them to see the way of life in many different countries and formed an integral part of their education. What is not so widely known is that there was a reverse tide of travellers eager to see the delights that England had to offer. One of these was Carl Philip Moritz, a resident of Hamelin, in Germany, who came to England in 1782. His first impressions were of the Thames estuary, and were shared with a friend back at home:

The land creeps ever closer; the danger of the voyage is over now and we can begin to rest easy in our minds. How wonderful to stand once more between visible limits after being tossed so long upon a vast expanse! How safe and cosy does the wanderer feel in his nightly inn and the seafarer in the long-sought harbour! For a man may be surrounded by a vast horizon, though the monstrous sea is everywhere, yet he can think only of his immediate environment - of one small portion of the whole.

But it is a very superior portion of bounteous Nature which I see now. The Thames is dotted with many ships, large and small, sailing by or lying at anchor. The hills on either side are clothed in a green as mild and soft as ever I saw. The banks of the Elbe from which I came are as much surpassed by these as autumn is by spring. Everywhere about me I can see only fruitful land. The quickset hedges which enclose the cornfields give this country scene the aspect of a great majestic garden. Neat villages and pretty little towns lie here and there, with the graceful country houses of the gentry in between, all betokening a state of comfortable well-being.

Especially fine is the view towards Gravesend, cleverly built on the side of a slope and around which hill and valley, fields and hedgerows are pleasantly intermingled with the parks and country houses; and there on one of the highest hills stands a windmill, a prominent landmark seen by the sailors in its familiar setting from various points along the winding Thames.

But since no pleasure ever comes undiluted, so we on the quarterdeck are at the mercy of the weather. This is cold and turbulent. A long sharp shower has driven me into the cabin where I am trying to brighten a dull hour by writing to you about a pleasant one.

This morning the six of us who shared the captain's cabin asked to be put ashore a little before the ship reached Dartford, which is about ten English miles from London. This is the usual course taken by those who sail up the Thames, because of the astonishing mass of sea-borne traffic growing more and more congested as the City is approached. Often it takes several days for a ship to work its passage through those last few miles. Passengers who therefore wish to lose no time and to avoid such other inconveniences as frequent stops and buffeting by other craft, prefer to travel the last few miles by land, possibly in a post-chaise, the cost of which is not very dear, especially if three persons share the same vehicle, for then the three pay no more than one. This is allowed by Act of parliament.

A rousing cheer went up for us from the German crew of our ship, after the fashion they have copied from the English sailors. The shore where we disembarked was white and chalky. We had to get to Dartford on foot, first going up a fairly steep hill which brought us straight from the river to our first English village. With this I was pleasantly surprised - with the neatness of its domestic architecture, red brick walls and flat roofs - especially when I compared these with the huts of our Prussian peasantry.

So we trailed along from one village to another like a caravan, each with his staff. Several people meeting us stared as if surprised by our appearance and manner of progress. We went by a small wood where a group of gipsies had encamped round a fire under a tree. The countryside grew ever more beautiful as we went our solitary way. The earth is not the same everywhere. How different did I find these living hedges, the green of them and of the trees - this whole paradisiacal region - from ours and all the others that I have seen! How incomparable the roads! How firm the pathway beneath me! With every step I took I was aware I trod on English ground!

Carl Philip Moritz, Journeys of a German in England in 1782, *Cape, 1965*

George III visits Maidstone

As a member of the Isle of Thanet troop of Yeomanry, under the command of Capt. Thomas Garrett, consisting of sixty members, we joined the Kentish troops of Yeomanry, on the 1st August, to be reviewed by His Majesty, George the Third, in the Moat Park, Maidstone, where there were assembled 6,000 Volunteers; a most glorious sight. The Royal Family, the Right Hon. W. Pitt, etc., etc., consisting of the nobility from all parts, who, with the troops and foot Volunteers, were most splendidly entertained by the Right Hon. The Earl of Romney, the proprietor of the Moat Park and Estate, and Lord Lieutenant of the county.

The length of the tables were 13,333 feet, placed on the ground in the Park; and the number of dishes were as follows: -

60 Lambs in quarters, making 240 dishes

700 Fowls, three in a dish

300 Hams

300 Tongues

220 Dishes of boiled beef

220 ditto, roasted

220 ditto, meat pies

220 Joints of Veal

7 Pipes of port wine bottled off

16 Butts of ale, beside plenty of table beer, placed in a vessel with a pump.

We all very much enjoyed this gratifying sight, it being a fine day, except a heavy shower which came soon after we left the Park, and which, as a matter of course, drenched some thousands of men and women, coming so unexpectedly as to prevent any escape.

His Majesty having expressed his sentiments of the good conduct, loyalty, and military efficiency of the troops, enlivened our spirits, in addition to the plentiful good cheer; so that many returned happily to their respective homes singing 'GOD SAVE THE KING'.

The day after, a wagon load of the fragments was carried to Maidstone, and there distributed to the poor of 600 families.

Mockett's Journal, 1799

[Later, a memorial pavilion was erected to commemorate the Royal Visit, and this may still be seen in Mote Park.]

Samuel Pepys at Chatham and Maidstone

In March 1669 Samuel Pepys, diarist and secretary to the Admiralty, paid a visit to Kent. Whilst it was navy business that really brought him to the county he took time for socialising and travel, visiting lady friends and his Admiralty colleague, Sir John Banks, who lived at The Friars, Aylesford. Later he took a meal at The Bell Inn, Maidstone, which stood at the top of Gabriel's Hill, and visited Kit's Coty House, the megalithic monument on the slopes of Bluebell Hill.

23rd. I took lunch with Commissioner Middleton, Captain Tinker, and Mr Huchinson, and out towards Chatham, and dined at Dartford, where we stayed an hour or two, it being a cold day; and so on, and got to Chatham just at night, with very good discourse by the way, but mostly of matter of religion, wherein Huchinson his vein lies. After supper we fell to talk of spirits and apparitions, whereupon many pretty particular stories were told, so as to make me almost afraid to lie alone, but for shame I could not help it; and so to bed; and, being sleepy, fell soon to rest, and so rested well.

24th . To the Hill House, and there did give order for a coach to be made ready; and got Mr Gibson, whom I carried with me, to go with me and Mr Coney, the surgeon, towards Maidstone, which I had a mighty mind to see, and took occasion, in my way, at St. Margett's to pretend to see Captain Allen, to see whether Mrs Jewkes, his daughter, was there; and there his wife came to the door, he being at London, and, through a window, I spied Jewkes, but took no notice of her, but made excuse till night, and then promised to come and see Mrs Allen again. A mighty cold and windy, but clear, day; and had the pleasure of seeing the Medway running, winding up and down mightily, and a very fine country; and I went a little out of the way to have visited Sir John Bankes, but he at London; but here I had a sight of his seat and house, the outside, which is an old abbey just like Hinchingbroke, and as good at least, and mighty finely placed by the river; and he keeps the grounds about it, and walls and the house, very handsome; I was mightily pleased with the sight of it. Thence to Maidstone, which I had a mighty mind to see, having never been there; and walked all up and down the town, and up to the top of the steeple, and had a noble view, and then down again; and in the town did see an old man beating of flax, and did step into the barn and give him money, and saw that piece of husbandry which I never saw, and it is very pretty; in the street also I did buy and send to our inn, The Bell, a dish of fresh fish. And so, having walked all round the town, and found it very pretty as most towns I ever saw, though not very big, and people of good fashion in it, we to our inn, and had a good dinner; and a barber came to me, and there trimmed me, that I might be clean against night, to go to Mrs. Allen. And so, staying till four o'clock, we set out, I alone in the coach going and coming; and in our way back, I 'light out of the way to see a Saxon monument, as they say, of a King, which is of three stones standing upright, and a great round one lying on them, of great bigness, although not so big as those on Salisbury Plain; but certainly it is a thing of great antiquity, and I am mightily glad to see it; it is near to Aylesford, where Sir John Bankes, lives. So homeward to Chatham, to Captain Allen's, and there 'light, and sent the coach and Gibson home, and I and Coney stayed; and there comes to us Mrs Jewkes, who is a very fine proper lady as most I know, and well dressed. Here was also a gentlemen, one Major Manly, and his wife, neighbours; and here we stayed, and drank, and talked, and sat. Coney and he to play while Mrs Jewkes and I to talk, and there had all our old stories up, and there I had the liberty to salute her often; and she mighty free in kindness to me; and had there been time, I might have carried her to Cobham, as she, upon my proposing it, was very willing to go. Here was a pretty cousin of hers come in to supper also, of a great fortune, daughter-in-law to this Manly, mighty pretty, but had now such a cold, she could not speak. Here stayed till almost twelve at night, and then with a lantern from thence walked over the fields, as dark as pitch, and mighty cold, and snow, to Chatham, and Mr Coney with great kindness to me; and there all in bed before I came home, and so I presently to bed.

The Diary of Samuel Pepys, *Macmillan, 1935*

Chatham and Faversham

Tuesday 15th May 1759

After Breakfast went to Chatham about two miles, Saw the Dock and yards. A Review there of a Number of Soldiers made a good Appearance as wee past. Was upon Board a Valliant a Man of warr then building, Had many things explained to Us in the Yards by Mr Hughes, known to Mr Mount, and wee had the pleasure of being present in the Smith's Shop at the Instant the severall workmen were turning an Anchor of a Man of warr of 4 ton weight then in the fire; All our Attentions were engrossed, as it was a Surprizing thing, and wee were fill'd with horror at the glowing heat of the severall furnaces, and at the Appearance of the Workmen, who with great Dexterity managed the affair; Anchors are made by hammering piece upon piece. Refreshed ourselves at the Rose at Sittingbourn. The Assembly is kept here, a good Room and Conveniency for Musick. Din'd at the Red Lyon at Ospring which is 18 miles. One Mr March of Faversham joined Us, being an Acquaintance of Mr Mounts. Made Us Laugh with his Ya-Haws etc. Politely invited Us to Tea at his house, and showed us the way to the Decoy ponds near Faversham. We were much pleased with the walk, and tho' Mr Mount and Mrs Hunt chose to ride, yet the party occasionally met; Were Instructed in the manner Wild Ducks are taken, and had Tea at Mr March's at Faversham - which is a pretty clean Village. Then sat out for Canterbury which is 9 Miles. This evening Mr Goodwin had the Blue Devils strong upon Him, a Disorder occasion'd by Various Causes. He went to bed early, had the honor of a Visit from the Ladies, and to his great mortification, put them to the Rout, by Instantly jumping out of bed to receive Them.

'A Tour into Kent', Berkshire Record Office, D/Amt F5

The Hazards of the Charabanc

These two accounts show the perils of early open-topped buses which had trouble with our many steep Kentish hills.

WESTERHAM

In the 1920s an open-topped double-decker bus, number 410, ran through Westerham. If it rained there were tarpaulin covers supplied which you could draw up under your chin, or even hide under completely. When the bus went under a bridge the conductor would come up the stairs and shout "Mind your heads" and we all ducked down low to avoid being decapitated.

Another bus we sometimes travelled by was the single-decker bus up from Crockham Hill. Sometimes this bus just could not manage the steep hill coming up from Crockham Hill to Kent Hatch, and then all the passengers had to get out and walk up the hill and the bus waited for them at the top. One very hot day when we had walked up we found there was a Walls "stop me and buy one" ice cream man at the top with his tricycle. So everyone, including the driver and conductor, bought an ice cream. Good business for the ice cream man.

WILMINGTON

When I was a child at Wilmington, I remember having to get off the bus when it could not make it to the top of Church Hill. When the passengers were all off, the conductor would put a wooden block behind the back wheels to stop the bus running back down the hill. Then the passengers would help to push the bus over the brow of the hill to flatter ground. On occasions the driver would drive off leaving some passengers behind.

At the bottom of the hill the trees growing either side made an archway across the road. In the winter there were just bare branches but in the summer, when the trees were in full leaf, it was a beautiful sight. The only drawback was, as the buses were open-topped, if it was or had been raining, you had to duck to keep from getting wet.

West Kent in Living Memory, *Countryside Books, 1988*

4 · ACCIDENTS

So often it is the unusual, rather than the mundane that is committed to paper. Everyday occurrences are, by implication, always going to happen so they are not recorded. Here is a selection of weird and wonderful things that were seen as so strange at the time that someone felt they should be committed to paper – from freak weather to accidents and disasters caused by man.

A Shower of Hay

This letter was written by the Bishop of Rochester from his Manor at Bromley in July 1797, and describes a remarkable meteorological phenomenon.

Sir, The forenoon of this day was remarkably sultry, with little sunshine, except for about two hours and a half from noon. The greatest heat was about 3 o'clock, when the sky was overcast again. At that time the thermometer already in the shade, at a window on the north side of my house, and so fixed as to face the east, was at 81 degrees. But a little before it was taken at 77 degrees, and the Barometer, at the same time, which in the morning had been 30.08 was sunk at 30.03. Just about this time I observed the cows and Welsh poneys in my paddock all galloping towards the yard, as if something had frightened them. The sky was overcast with dark lowering clouds, the swallows were flying very low, and from many appearances I apprehended that a heavy thunderstorm was approaching. We had sitten down to dinner (perhaps about 5 or 10 minutes past four) when a young Lady at table suddenly exclaimed in great surprise, that 'the hay was all falling about the garden.' Running to the window I saw many little handfuls of hay falling gently and almost perpendicularly through the air upon my lawn. Going to the front door, I saw the same sort of shower descending upon the grass on the contrary side of the house, and found my gardener and labourers gazing at it. I observed a large black cloud coming over the house with a very slow motion from south to north, or nearly in that direction. Fixing my eyes steadily on the middle of that cloud, I saw several of these parcels of hay, one after another, dropping in appearance from the bosom of the cloud, and becoming first visible at a great height in the atmosphere. They descended with a very slow motion, and with a very small deviation from the perpendicular in the direction in which the cloud moved. The atmosphere all this time was remarkably close and still. Not a leaf of the trees moved, not a breath of air was stirring, and my own hay was lying motionless in the field. Towards the evening a light breeze sprang up, which soon died away again; and the whole day has passed off without thunder, rain or storm of any kind. The specimen of this hay, which I have the honour to send to you, is the aggregate of two of the little parcels picked up by myself on opposite sides of the house.

I have the honour to be, Sir,

With great respect

Your most obedient

Very Hnble Servant,

ROCHESTER

A Mottingham Dene Hole

This account is probably of a Dene Hole – a medieval chalk mine that had been abandoned and forgotten – and which had opened up after heavy rain.

In 1585, at Mottingham, near Eltham, in a Field belonging to Sir Peter Hart, the ground began to sink so that three great Elms were swallowed up, the tops falling downward into the hole, and no more could be discerned, the place being filled with water; the compass of the whole was about 80 yards, and a sounding line of 50 Fathom could find no bottom.

Ten yards distant another piece of ground sank near the Highway, so nigh a dwelling house that the inhabitants were greatly terrified.

Admirable Curiosities, Rarities and Wonders in Great Britain and Ireland, *1718*

The Great Storm of 1763

On Friday, August 19th, 1763, a storm arose at sea, off the Sussex coast. The morning was still, with scarcely a breeze of air; and so excessively hot, that it was suffocating. About ten o'clock in the forenoon, a black cloud arose towards the west; soon after which the wind blew an hurricane: the clouds came on with amazing velocity, throwing out in their course dreadful flashes of lightning; and the thunder was almost one continual roar. About half-past eleven, the rain poured in torrents, and in a few minutes was intermixed with some detached hailstones, which were very large, as introductory of what were to follow; the hail, wind, lightning and thunder, soon came on so furiously, that all was one dreadful scene of horror. The boughs, branches and leaves of trees, broken and stript off, flying in the wind, still more darkened the air; the tiles and windows rattling, and dashing to pieces; trees torn up, and falling, struck all with a terror not easily to be expressed; some running distractedly about, wringing their hands, while others stood like inanimate beings. The storm lasted about half-an-hour. What a scene ensued! An universal desolation everywhere presented itself: some houses filled with water; others, with their barns blown down; roofs and walls shattered; the windows quite destroyed; the waters pouring in torrents down the streets, plowing up the stones in their course, and leaving deep chasms: the surface of the earth covered with the prodigious hailstones and water; corn, fruit and hops destroyed; the fields and hop gardens everywhere disfigured; trenches formed by the rushing water; the roots of the hops bared, and the poles thrown down in all directions; heaps of stone and sand driven through the hedges; boughs and branches scattered; the fruit trees stripped of their bark. The smaller animals such as hares, pheasants and other game, lay dead in the fields; and a large hog was killed by the hail upon Barming Heath. The larger quadrupeds, endowed with superior instinct, saw their danger; horses, bullocks, and sheep ran and sheltered themselves from the coming storm. In Maidstone, on one side of the High Street, not only the glass, but the lead and frames of the windows were forced in and destroyed, particularly by the hail. It was like fragments of ice, and of very irregular shapes; at Barming, one piece was taken up formed like an oyster; Sir Philip Boteler measured it, and found it nine inches round at the extremity; and even ten days after, some hailstones were taken up four inches and a half in circumference. One of the largest struck the stile of an horizontal post-dial of brass, and bent it near thirty degrees towards the east. Posts, bars, and gates had deep impressions from them. They were of different shapes; some flat, irregular, and very much jagged; others an assemblage of pieces of ice; whilst a few were globular, with a small cavity in the centre; and if they were held together they immediately froze, and were not easily separated. The storm commenced in this county at Tunbridge Wells, whilst the people were at prayers in the chapel, and passed quite across to Sheerness, a distance of forty miles, its breadth not exceeding four miles; the direction of it was from south-west by west, to north-east by east; and it was severely felt in the parishes of Tunbridge, Speldhurst, Penshurst, Tudely, Capel, Pembury, part of Hadlow, Yalding, Hunton, Brenchley, Mereworth, East and West Farleigh, Wateringbury, East and West Peckham, Nettlestead, East Malling, Teston, Barming, Loose, Maidstone, Boxley and Detling; after which its violence was spent, and only little injury was occasioned. Numbers came from all parts to witness the melancholy scene. The inhabitants of the vicinity humanely raised £3000 in a few months, which in some measure relieved the unhappy sufferers: but the cruel effects long remained: most of the hop-hills died: the filbert and apple trees swelled in knots where they had been bruised: and some were so injured, that the branches and shoots long after continued to die; the cherry trees bore it the best, owing perhaps to the strength of their outward bark.

The Revd Mark Noble, Rector of Barming, in Brayley's Beauties of England and Wales, *1815.*

The Big Flood

I lay there in the big double bed, my rubber ring tucked under one arm, my favourite doll and swimming hat held tightly in the other. I was nine years old, not yet able to swim, absolutely terrified but ready for the worst! I have to smile and relate this story when the subject of the 'big flood of the 1950s' comes up in conversation, because lying there in that big bed is one of the most vivid memories of that terrifying time.

Other memories are of my dear Aunty, who slept downstairs, being woken by the wall-plug by her bed going 'pop'. She swung her feet out of bed into water, ankle deep. Of my sister wading through the house with water up to her waist, rescuing cats and handing a bucket of coal and a kettle of water and the tea tray up to us on the stairs. Of one of the cats sailing by on a rug, so terrified and wet, to be plucked to safety. Of lighting the fire in my bedroom and boiling the kettle for 'a nice cup of tea', and making toast. How grateful we were that my Aunty always stuck to her wartime routine of getting everything ready for the next day before going to bed.

When daylight finally came, the water was almost up to the ceilings downstairs. We had a verandah on the front of the house and I shall never forget the sight of Nurse Jones clambering out of a rowing boat and onto the verandah. My Aunty had to have two injections a day and our lovely nurse was not going to let her down.

Late that day the long boat came down our street and collected us all. I don't remember much of that trip except I was wearing pyjamas under three jumpers and two shirts, topped with a coat, hat and wellies. There wasn't room for suitcases!

It was a few days before the water went and my last memory brings the biggest smile - as we walked back into the devastation of our home I was told to tread carefully because of the inches of slimy mud covering everything. What did I do? One step inside, my toes came up and I landed on my bottom in all that horrid mud!

East Kent within Living memory, *Countryside Books, 1995*

The Wreck of the Margate

The dreadful catastrophe of the foundering of the Corn Hoy, called the 'Margate', belonging to Mr. John Sackett, of that place, happened in the night of the 6th of February, 1802. She was deeply laden with corn for the London market, and had 29 passengers, besides the crew of four men. They sailed about three o'clock in the afternoon of Saturday, and about eleven o'clock at night she struck upon one of the banks below Reculver's sand when she became totally unmanageable.

In this perilous condition they tried every effort to save the ship; three feet of water was in the hold; and she came on her broadside to the beach, which occasioned her to sink.

The following is an account of the persons on board when the vessel stranded:-

Persons drowned:

Mr. John Goodbourn, Captain

Mr George Bone, Carpenter

Mr Henry Thornton and his wife, together with their son aged 19 years

Mrs Crow, a widow

Mrs Field, a widow; with others amounting to 23

Persons saved:

Mr John Carroway, Margate

Mr Nuckell, Broadstairs

Mr Field, ditto

John Busbridge, St.Peter's

NB A subscription was made by the gentlemen of Margate, for those in need of assistance, and on the 25th March £350 was collected.
Mockett's Journal, *1802*

1665 Great Storm

1665, at Deal, on November 14, 15, 16 and 17, (both day and night) the storm continued, with much hail. At Dover, a circumstance happened, not unworthy of notice:- Sir Arthur Kingsley's Prize was so beaten by the waves, that three of his men were washed overboard by one sea; their lives were saved by another wave, which threw them back into their ship, with a dead man in their company. A volume would not contain a narrative of the sad effects throughout the Kingdom; the loss of human life, and damage done to cathedrals, churches, steeples, houses, trees, etc . . .

Nov 14th. At Chatham church, the lead was rolled up together, and blown off to twenty yards distance; in fact, it is stated that eleven hundred and seven houses in Kent, were blown down; orchard and other trees, destroyed.
17th. At Hawkhurst, eleven barns were blown down; all the windmills in town and country were blown down.
26th. There were twelve ships of war lost, and 1611 men, with 524 guns.

'Prepare ye to hear
  The Worst report that ever reached your ear -
  One friend may mollify another's grief,
  But public loss admits of no relief.'

The *Restoration* lost 386 men and 70 guns; the *Northumberland*, 253 men; the *Mary*, 272 men.
Mockett's Journal, *1788*

A Tragedy at Broadstairs

A very awful circumstance occurred near the harbour, at Broadstairs, on the 14th of January. One of the boats of that place having been to sea, for the purpose of assisting a ship in distress, had the misfortune to upset as it returned, between seven and eight o'clock in the evening, (being very dark), when the four following persons were drowned:- Oldfield, Simpson, Bayley, and Langley; by which sad event, three widows and sixteen children had to lament the loss of their protectors, and were left in great distress.
It is singular, that three of the Oldfield family were drowned near Broadstairs, on former occasions, viz.:
William Oldfield, March 16th, 1783,Aged 55 years
John, son of ditto, Nov. 25th, 1790, aged 25 years

William, bro of ditto, Feb. 14th, 1812, aged 58 years

John, son of ditto, Jan. 14th 1828, aged 32 years

The family of Bayley has frequently met the same unfortunate fate, by assisting ships in distress. Both families were remarkable, for being exceedingly good seamen.

An extraordinary circumstance occurred in the fate of the first Oldfield. His body was anxiously enquired for at every part of the coast, and a reward offered, but without success, until about four months after, when a pair of large silver shoe-buckles (such as sailors usually wore) were observed by a neighbour in passing over Sandwich bridge. He asked a person who had them on, some questions, and found that they were Oldfield's, which led to the further discovery, that a fisherman had picked the body up, and after taking between five and six pounds from his pockets, his clothes from his back, and the shoes and buckles from his feet, he buried him, in the sand near Deal. The man who found Oldfield was rewarded; the corpse was taken by his friends, and buried on 17th July, in St. Peter's churchyard; and on his headstone are some verses, the beginning of which are as follow:

'Though boisterous waves, and stormy winds,

Have tossed me to and fro -

Yet by the force of God's decree,

I harbour here below.'

The bodies of John Bayley and Robert Simpson, were the first buried in St. Peter's new burial ground. The others were interred in the old church-yard, on the 20th Jan. 1828

Mockett's Journal, *1828*

Mr Henry Hawkes is Saved by his Dog

Mr Henry Hawkes, a farmer residing at Halling, in Kent, was late one evening at Maidstone market. On returning at night, with his dog, who was usually at his heels, he again stopped at Aylesford, and as is too frequently the case upon such occasions, he drank immoderately, and left the place in a state of intoxification. Having passed the village of New heed (Newhythe) in safety, he took his way over Snodland Brook - in the best season of the year a very dangerous road for a drunken man. The whole face of the country was covered with deep snow, and the frost intense. He had, however, proceeded in safety till he came to the Willow Walk, within half a mile of the church, when by a sudden stagger he quitted the path, and passed over on his right hand. Not apprehensive he was going astray, he took towards the river; but having a high bank to mount, and being nearly exhausted with wandering and the effect of the liquor, he was most fortunately prevented from rising the mound, or he certainly must have precipitated himself (as it was near high water) into the Medway.

At this moment, completely overcome, he fell among the snow in one of the coldest nights ever known, turning upon his back. He was soon overpowered by either sleep or cold, when his faithful defendant, who had closely attended to every step, scratched away the snow so as to throw up a sort of protecting wall around his helpless master; then mounting upon the exposed body, rolled himself round and lay upon his master's bosom, for which his shaggy coat proved a most seasonable covering, and eventual protection during the dreadful severity of the night, the snow falling all the time.

The following morning a person who was out with his gun, in expectation of falling in with some sort of wildfowl, perceiving an appearance somewhat uncommon, ventured to approach the spot; upon his coming up the dog got off the body, and after repeatedly shaking himself to get disentangled from the accumulated snow, encouraged the sportsman (a Mr Finch) by his actions of the most significant nature, to come near the side of his master. Upon wiping away the icy incrustation from the face, the countenance was immediately recollected; but, the frame appearing lifeless, assistance was procured to convey it to the first house upon the skirts of the village, when, a pulsation being observed, every possible means was instantly adopted to promote his recovery.

In the course of a short time the farmer was sufficiently restored to relate his own story, as already recited, and in gratitude for his miraculous escape ordered a silver collar to be made for his friendly protector, as a perpetual remembrance of the transaction. A gentleman of the faculty in the neighbourhood, hearing of the circumstance, and finding it so well authenticated, immediately made him an offer of ten guineas for the dog, which the grateful farmer refused, exultingly adding that so long as he had a bone to his meat, or crust to his bread, he would divide it with the faithful friend who had preserved his life: and this he did in a perfect conviction that the warmth of the dog, in covering the most vital part, had continued the circulation and prevented a total stagnation of the blood by the frigidity of the elements.

Edward Jesse, Gleanings in Natural History, *1842*

Church registers often give more information than the bare record of baptism, marriage, burial and date – helping us to flesh out the details of what would otherwise be a colourless record.

From the Offham Parish Register:

1800. Elizabeth Spearman, wife of Robert Spearman, overturned in the Chatham stage going to London, and killed on the spot in a moment; buried in Offham church, Dec. 26 aged 49. For burying in the church and putting up a memorial monument, I charged, and Mr. Spearman paid me, four guineas or £4 4s 0d. John Liptrott, rector of Offham.

From the Aylesford Parish Register:

Henry Gorham and John Allen, the one a bricklayer, and the other a carpenter's apprentice, going into ye river at Forman's forstall to wash them, being upon the xxvth day of June 1661, were both drowned, and were buried in two several graves in this churchyard, the xxviith day of ye said June, 1661.

From the Snodland Register:

1796. July 24th, John Taylor, aged 30 years, forced overboard by the foresail of Mr Bensted's barge, and drowned near the mouth of the creek.

Mishaps with Rockets

In consequence of a very serious accident last year, which happened to John Newby, (a lad in my service,) aged 15 years, by an explosion of gunpowder, in his pocket, and who now lives in a situation of most dreadful suffering, from the effects, (although twelve months since), the deputy, Mr Barfield, had hand-bills circulated to caution persons not to let off rockets, etc., stating the law against it. This, in some degree, had the desired effect in our parish; but in Margate, where there was no notice given, a similar accident happened to a young man named Smith. He was so much burnt, as to expire a short time after. To return to poor Newby; he continued in the greatest suffering from November 5th 1825 to February 10th 1827, before he could sit up in his bed, and on the 20th May, with assistance, he got down stairs; on the 29th, he was led out of the house for air; and on Sunday, the 17th June, he was at church to return thanks to Almighty God for his recovery. Much credit was due to Mr. Ketchley, surgeon, for his kind and unmerited attention to him. In 1828, he was apprenticed to Mr. Webb, shoemaker, and in 1833, he married, in London.

Mockett's Journal, *1833*

In Milton Regis Churchyard

Accidents with fireworks are nothing new. Here is a record of an accident only ninety years after the Gunpowder Plot which our celebrations commemorate.

Here lieth the
body of Simon
Gilker Junior
who was killed by
means of a rockett
November 5th 1696
Aged 48 years

Dickens' witnesses the Kent Railway Disaster of 1865

Dickens was involved in a well-publicised railway crash in Kent in which ten people were killed and over fifty, including himself, injured. This extract is not recommended for late night-time reading.

At the end of May (1865), Dickens went to Paris for a week's vacation. It is probable that Ellen Ternan was with him on this brief holiday; it is certain that she returned with him. While there Dickens picked up rapidly. 'before I went away,' he wrote Mary, 'I certainly worked myself into a damaged state. But the moment I got away, I began, thank God, to get well.'

The 9th of June, the day of their return, was clear and beautiful. Steamers could enter Folkestone Harbour only at high tide, which that day was a little after two. Dickens and Ellen boarded the 'tidal' train, and a little later they were spinning along the rails at fifty miles and hour.

At eleven minutes past three the train entered on a straight stretch of track between Headcorn and Staplehurst. One third of the way there came a slight dip in the level country to a stream bed crossed by a railway bridge of girders. Suddenly the driver clamped on the brakes, reversed his engine, and whistled for the guards to apply their hand brakes. He had seen a flagman with a red flag and a gap of ripped-up rails.

A crew of repairmen were carrying on a routine replacement of worn timbers, but their foreman had looked at the time-table for the next day and imagined that the train would not be along for another two hours. The flagman was supposed to be 1,000 yards beyond the gap and to have laid down fog signals, but that day he had neglected the signals and was only 550 yards from the bridge. When the engineer saw him it was too late. As he reached the bridge the train was still going almost thirty miles and hour.

The engine leaped the 42-foot gap in the rails and ran to the farther bank of the river bed. The guard's van that followed was flung to the parallel track, dragging the next coach with it. The coach immediately behind was that in which Dickens and Ellen were seated. It jolted partly over the side of the bridge, ten feet above the stream, with its rear end in the field below. The other coaches ran down the bank, turning upside down in the marshy ground, where four of them were smashed to matchwood. Only the very rear of the train remained on the rails.

'Suddenly,' Dickens said, 'we were off the rail, and beating the ground as the car of a half-emptied balloon might do.' Dickens clambered out the window to obtain help in opening the door. Standing on the step, he saw the timbers of the bridge gone and the river ten feet below. Two guards were running wildly up and down. Dickens called authoritatively to one of them and demanded the key that would open the carriage doors. With the aid of a labourer and a few planks, he brought Ellen to safety and freed the occupants of the other compartments,

Then he went back for his brandy flask, filled his hat with water, and began trying to help the injured and the dying. Remains of the shattered carriages were projecting wheels-upwards from the water. The screams of the sufferers were appalling. A staggering man covered with blood had 'such a frightful cut across the skull,' Dickens said, 'that I couldn't bear to look at him. I poured some water over his face, gave him some drink, then gave him some brandy, and laid him down in the grass . . .' One lady, who had been crushed to death was laid on the bank just as her husband, screaming 'My wife! My wife!' rushed up and found her a mangled corpse. Dickens was everywhere, helping everyone.

When he had done everything he could, he remembered that he had had the manuscript of the next number of *Our Mutual Friend* with him, and coolly climbed into the carriage to retrieve it. Only when he was back at Gad's Hill did he realize how shaken he was. His hand was so unsteady that to most of the inquiries that poured in about his health he dictated his replies. But her nerved himself to write the Station Master at Charing Cross on Ellen's behalf:

A lady who was in the carriage with me in the terrible accident on Friday, lost, in the struggle of being got out of the carriage, a gold watch-chain with a smaller gold watch-chain attached, a bundle of charms, a gold watch-key, and a gold seal engraved 'Ellen.' I promised the lady to make her loss known at headquarters, in case these trinkets should be found.

Throughout the month Dickens was unable to throw off the effects of the accident. 'I am curiously weak - weak as if I were recovering from a long illness,' he told Forster. And a little later, ' I begin to feel it more in my head. I sleep well and eat well; but I write half a dozen notes, and turn faint and sick.' 'I am getting right, though still low in pulse and very nervous. Driving into Rochester yesterday I felt more shaken than I have since the accident.'

In his weakness and shock he did not forget about Ellen. Solicitously he sent her little delicacies by John, his personal servant. 'Take Miss Ellen tomorrow morning, a little basket of fresh fruit, a jar of clotted cream from Tuckers, and a chicken, a pair of pigeons, or some nice little bird. Also on Wednesday morning, and on Friday morning, take her some other things of the same sort - making a little variety each day.'

At the end of June, 'I cannot bear railway travelling yet,' Dickens wrote Forster. Indeed, he never fully recovered. 'To this hour,' he wrote over three years later, 'I have sudden vague rushes of terror, even when riding in a hansom cab . . .'. For a while he could bear railway travel only by slow trains, but long journeys and boredom were worse than the tension of the express. It became his invariable habit, however, to carry a flask of brandy with him. 'My reading secretary and companion knows so well when one of these odd momentary seizures come upon me in a railway carriage, that he instantly produces a dram of brandy, which rallies the blood to the heart and generally prevails.' Even so, when the train jolted over intersections, he often clutched the arms of his chair, his face whitened, and his brow broke out in perspiration.

Edgar Johnson, Charles Dickens, His tragedy and triumph, *Allen Lane, 1952*

5 · FARMING

Kent - the Garden of England. This well-known description has been in use for hundreds of years, underlining Kent's reputation as the source of much of London's vegetables and fruit. Market gardening in east Kent, orchards and hop gardens in the west, and smallholdings in between – this is still the pattern of agriculture in what is quickly becoming an increasingly industrial region. Many of these extracts reflect a romanticised views of farming, but I have tried to contrast them with others suggesting that all was not as rosy as the traditional view proclaims.

Wheels of Progress

Joan Kent writes about her childhood in rural Kent just before the Second World War.

Services that people in urban areas took for granted were extremely slow in reaching outlying districts such as ours. We knew that, given time, the wheels of progress must inevitably turn in our direction, although they always tended to get bogged down and broken-axled on their way.

So infrequent were the changes in our way of living that the importance of the most mundane inventions tended to become magnified out of all proportion. The siting of the first telephone box in the parish caused as much excitement as if it had descended from the sky.

It was arranged that as soon as the Post Office engineers had connected it, the chairman of the parish council would declare it officially open, and make the first formal phone call to the mayor of the nearby market town. It all proved to be a bit of an anti-climax, because by the time our parish chairman had changed his gumboots and driven his milk lorry over to Plough Lane corner, the kiosk was already in use. The innkeeper's layabout son was in there holding a long and acrimonious argument with his bookie, and even when he finished, Tom Grommett's wife was standing belligerently by the kiosk door.

She had arrived first, and anyone who tried to stop her phoning her sister would get the rough side of her tongue. It took some time for Mrs Grommett to receive a stitch-by-stitch detail of her sister's major abdominal operation.

Our local dignitary was getting impatient and hammered on the kiosk door, but having invested sixpence in phoning her sister Mrs Grommett was determined to use every second she had bought. Six pennies in those days bought a lot of telephone time.

When the chairman was finally free to declare the kiosk open his only audience were the ducks and geese that had waddled over from the pond on the off-chance of being fed.

Two passengers alighting from the market day bus displayed no interest at all. Even the formality of his official phone call had to be cut short when he discovered that he had only one penny to be swallowed by Button A.

The mayor he was phoning was an auctioneer by profession, so cutting the social niceties to a minimum our local chairman took the opportunity to discover the latest selling price for barren cows and in-calf heifers, before the line went dead.

Although power cables had begun to etch black lines above our lanes and hedgerows, none of the houses in the village had been connected to mains power supply. So the fact that it was illuminated by electricity made the new phone box unique.

That one small, harsh light seemed to shine out like a beacon in the darkness at the far end of the unlit village. It attracted moths and maybugs and on Friday and Saturday evenings the lads and lasses of the village used to congregate within the circle of its light.

Girls, whose parents believed any artificial aids to beauty were snares of the devil and forbade their daughters to use make-up, took advantage of the illuminated mirror above the telephone directory shelf to try out the lipstick and powder they would never dare to apply in the candle-lit bedrooms of their homes.

The old saddler in Plough Cottage found that the phone box saved him money. On dark evenings, when the weather was not too bad, he would take his stool, a newspaper, and his glasses, and settle down in the phone box for a quiet read.

There were those who felt sure there must be some law forbidding such practice, but he would always willingly vacate it if someone wanted to make a call.

As he said, it was a darn sight less draughty to sit in than Plough Cottage and the light bulb certainly made reading easier than did a smoky lamp.

'There's folk what are jealous because they don't live handy enough to take advantage of new inventions, as I can', he would tell his critics. And in their hearts they knew him to be right.

Not everyone was sure that the arrival of electricity in the village was a good thing. To be able to make light and heat without flame or fire smacked of dark practices.

Deep down superstitions made the older generations extremely wary of the invisible power that lay in cold wires obeying switches, yet could kill a man in much the same way as lightning in a storm.

Fear of electricity caused old Grandfather Chapple, the dairyman, to put a spoke in the wheels of progress, making for months of litigation and legal argument, because he was convinced that if the authorities put power lines across his pastures the dairy herd grazing beneath them were in constant danger of curdling their milk.

Progress was slow in other directions. If The Season's Collection meant high fashion and dress shows to town dwellers, in our language it meant the quarterly visit of the rubbish-collecting cart.

My father held a contract to provide a driver, horse and wagon to accompany two council employees to each dwelling in the parish, four times a year.

One might well believe that with thirteen weeks between each visit the village would be inundated with refuse, but in fact very little was collected on the rounds.

Almost everything we used seemed to be disposable, serving as fuel for the open fires, food for backyard fowls, or compost for the garden. Even tins served as rut fillers where iron banded cart wheels cut deep into unmade tracks.

Iron bedsteads were traditional materials for cottage garden fence mending. Old discarded matresses were dug into the soil to improve its tilth. Rags served the same purpose, unless they were sold to the old rag-and-bone man who travelled around the area with a creaking cart and a skinny pony.

It was considered perfectly honourable to inspect other people's rubbish heaps just before collection day in case they were discarding any article for which one could perhaps find a use.

Children, too, found this to be a profitable pastime, collecting empty bottles and returning them to the back door of the Hare and Hounds, at a penny a time.

The vicarage rubbish was sacrosanct, but when the parson's sister hid the evidence of her 'little falling' by disposing of the empties down the burrows of a rabbit warren up on Lockley Bank, we all knew there would be no profit there.

Nothing was considered too large or too small to be carried away by the collectors, but errors were sometimes made. Their round went as far as Tyler's End Cottage, where a cantankerous old man lived with a daughter whom he brow-beat into believing that the shock of her engagement had made him unable to walk.

For years she pushed him around in a whicker bathchair, until the collectors found it by the cottage rubbish heap and carried it away. The old man walked two miles to retrieve it, and pushed it, buckle-wheeled, the two miles back.

A month later he walked his daughter up the aisle.

One day a steam lorry delivered twelve gross of toilet rolls and a huge drum of disinfectant to our farm. Dad had no knowledge where it came from but the council sanitary inspector told him to distribute it all around the village when the next collection took place.

Toilet rolls were a complete innovation, making excellent tracing paper and, with health hints printed all over them, much too interesting to waste.

Not everyone was happy to receive the free samples and some even more unhappy with the results. The old saddler, meeting Dad in the village, said so, but Dad replied it was a sign of advancing progress to try to kill off germs.

'Progress, be blowed!' said the saddler. 'I put some of that stuff in my old bucket and emptied it on the garden. If that's progress... it's killed off all my beans.'

Joan Kent, Wood Smoke and Pigeon Pie, *Bailey Brothers and Swinfen Ltd, 1977*

Mechanisation comes to Kent

The social and financial changes brought about by mechanisation in the agricultural industry in the early nineteenth century were not universally popular as Mockett recorded in his Journal.

September 28th (1830), in consequence of the labouring classes having suffered very much from want of employment, and being under the necessity of applying for parochial assistance, they were induced to meet on Barham Downs, under the impression that the machines, called thrashing machines, were principally the means of depriving them of work. Upwards of 200 persons assembled there, and resolved to proceed to Dover, Deal, Ash, Wingham etc., to destroy them. These measures were put into execution, and they visited the several places by day light and destroyed them. This was followed by incendiary fires. Mr Michael Becker, of Goldston, Ash, had his corn stacks burnt, to the value of £3,000; (they were insured.) The Rev. Ralph Price, of Lyminge, suffered very much. Several hay stacks were burnt; and fires occurred almost every night in Kent, so that in this and almost every other parish, a large number of special constables were sworn in. Many persons protected their property by watching their premises themselves.

Nov. 15th, a large sanfoine hay stack was consumed on Alland Grange, belonging to George Hannam, Esq.

Nov. 30th, at the East Kent Special Sessions, Canterbury, on the 26th, Henry Andrews and Thomas Stroud, were sentenced to be transported for seven years; and Thomas Read, for life; for breaking machines at Wingham.

John Stonward and William Stone, seven years; James Dowker and

Henry Hulkes, seven years each; John Friday and several others, a less punishment.

Although I never had a thrashing machine, nor do I think I ever should, for many reasons, yet I see no cause why any man should not have his work performed in whatever manner he prefers; It is not to the interest of individuals to destroy, or resist by disgraceful and injurious outrages (such as have been committed) by burning the corn etc., as it must soon spread famine and desolation throughout the land.

The distress of the poor, occasioned from the want of employment, will greatly increase, if this horrible crime continues.

It will bring on their own heads, on their children, and their fellow creatures, evils which will terrify the stoutest hearts, and fill with repentance and remorse, the boldest of their leaders.

Why should not the farmer be permitted to use the instrument to do his work called a machine? Suppose labourers were to go to a carpenter, and tell him he ought not to use a saw, because it cuts the wood so much better than if he split it, and thereby lessens that labour it would otherwise require.

There can be no difference between the case of the labourer who breaks the thrashing machine of the farmer, and that of the man who should destroy the saw, or other implements of the carpenter.

It is true, the number of labourers exceed the means of the farmer; but he does not, in general, employ the less by having a thrashing machine. It has been brought on by a train of circumstances; among others, overgrown population. But the remedy would not be found by employing two men to do that which one can do. The burthen of parochial taxes, the heavy charges of tradesmen, together with high rents, place the farmer in a situation that he cannot pay for as many labourers as he is really in want of, to cultivate his land with advantage to himself, the labourer; and the community.

Some persons say the thrashing machines save one tenth part of the grain. If it does, it is five week's consumption of the kingdom; the difference between a good, or a bad harvest, between a dear, and a cheap year; therefore, if they break all these machines, they do as much harm to the country as if they made a dearth in it.

Mockett's Journal, *1830*

Cherries

One of the Garden of England's crops is the cherry, the earliest reference to which dates from the fourteenth century. Here, a traditional ballad extols their virtue. Kentish Fire is the syncopated hand-clapping associated with football crowds and others today, but which originated as a communal sign of agreement here in Kent.

The maids of Kent, as well I know
Of all fair maids are fairest,
For on their pretty lips do grow
Ripe cherries of the rarest.
Red is the first uprising streak
Which opening day discloses;
Red is the blushing lover's cheek,
And red the blush of roses;
Red is the Christmas flame which glows
On glistening holly berries;
But of a richer red than those
Are lips of Kentish cherries.

Here's to the cherry lips of Kent,
Come fill your glasses higher
And toast them till the voice is spent,
With triple Kentish fire.
Sweet fruits grow 'neath another clime,
The orange, fig and melon,
The date, pomegranate, grape and lime
Are things one might well live on
But all these sweets of Nature's make
Or richest wines and sherries,
I'd gladly leave, one taste to take
Of those sweet Kentish cherries.

The Kentish Magazine, *1850 quoted in Alan Major 'Cherries in the Rise', S. B. Publications 1997*

Agriculture and Countryside

*Although Edward Blunden is known best as a First World War Poet,
he also wrote about his native county. He is commemorated by an
etched glass window by Laurence Whistler in his parish church of St.
Peter and St. Paul, Yalding.*

Come, for here the lazy night
With rosy camp-fires blossoms bright,
The stream half-runs with flute-like trill
Through the quaint channels of the mill
And, to accentuate the hush,
Through fine bamboo and needled rush
A water-spirit ferries. Come,
And see how kindly all's at home.
No sweeter things than these I rhyme,
And this by much their sweetest time.
The sweet, agree, and by this gate,
Watch each one gathering to his mate,
To nest or warren, bough or byre -
The dearness answers all desire,
When all, the shepherd, dog and sheep
With sleep-like motions welcome sleep;
The elm-tree's momentary stir
And freshened sluices yield to her,
And though the fire-side shout and song
'Defy her there, they will not be long.

The bonfire's crackling zeal dies down,
The laughing supper-groups are gone,
The fair falls quiet in Yalding town,
Alone with the mist I linger on.

Edmund Blunden, Poems of Many Years, *Collins, 1957*

The Oak in the Cherry Orchard

About a mile north-east of Sittingbourne is a very large and finely-planted cherry orchard, called East Hall cherry garden, and now in the occupation of Mr White, the proprietor. In the midst of the orchard is an oak tree, of considerable size and great beauty, which is literally growing in and supported by the trunk of an old cherry tree. The following history of this great curiosity is, I believe, authentic:

About the year 1789, Mr William Sneath, who then owned and occupied the premises, was walking with his wife in the orchard. As they passed a large cherry-tree, a rook flew out of a hollow place at the top of the trunk, where the branches begin to spread, about seven feet from the ground. On putting his hand into the place he felt something which he supposed to be an egg, but which proved to be an acorn, in the first stage of vegetation. "Don't destroy it," said Mrs Sneath, "it is unlucky to destroy an oak." In compliance with his wife's request, Mr Sneath replaced it in the same situation. There it speedily took root, and grew up, and has continued to flourish for forty-four years.

The lower part of the oak, where it first struck its roots into the top of the cherry tree, is now about three feet in circumference. The trunk of the oak is straight and well proportioned, and the branches for a head as finely shaped as any I remember to have seen. The branches of the cherry tree have long since perished, but the hole retains nearly its original shape, and is much more perfect than could have been expected, after the lapse of so many years. It appears, however, to be somewhat rent at the top, and the fibrous roots of the oaks have burst through the bark in several places, as if in search of soil to nourish them. If I am rightly informed, the oak is furnished with what is called a sap, or leading root, which strikes directly downwards, to a considerable depth, and thus increases the stability of the tree, by riveting it fast to the soil. If this be the case, the sap-root has, in all probability, made its way through the centre of the cherry-stalk, and found its natural aliment in the earth.

The Youth's Instructor, *July 1833*

Hops

Hops were first introduced to Kent by the Romans who used them as a vegetable, but the first recorded use of them in brewing was in 1514. Here the hop gardens and the annual competitions held between stringers are described by the manager of a country Inn.

It is generally agreed that though profitable, hops are one of the most expensive crops in the world to grow. There is first the heavy capital outlay of putting up the poles and wires. To give some idea of other costs, on a farm of fifty acres the bill for string or twine alone will come to well-nigh a thousand pounds, not a penny of which will be seen again. It is therefore not a bad idea if the worker who does the spring stringing is economical with the twine, and also it is an enormous advantage if he is quick. This, one assumes, is how and why these competitions got started, and why they are quite important.

This work must clearly be finished before the 'twiddlers' come on the scene, and it is quite fascinating watching a good stringer at work. Basically what he has to do is to get a continuous ball of string up to the wire trellises, which can be anything from sixteen to twenty-two feet high, and down again to a single hook on a 'hill'. This is the word for a single hop plant; the term is derived from the fact that in ancient days each plant was in fact cultivated on a minute hillock or mound of earth.

To do this the worker has a very long pole or rod, to which is attached a curved or angled piece of piping, through which the string is strung. The movement he is making while doing this is really quiet graceful, like a fly-fisher casting his rod. The pattern in which the string is hooked to the trellising will vary according to the type of hop selected or the growing policy of the owner. With the 'umbrella' system of wirework, the stringing is either 'upright' or 'cater' (cut diagonally). The latter way gives a longer run for the hop bine when the wirework is very low, and it does perhaps let in a little more light.

After the stringing comes the 'banding-in'. The 'bander-in' will generally be a woman and her job is to brace, or tie-in (with string) at breast height the four (usually) vertical strings which, as already explained, go from the trellises down to the hill. Actually, with 'upright' stringing, the four strings when brought together will form a nine-inch square, some four feet six inches above the ground.

The hop-stringing was organised by the Weald of Kent Ploughing Association, whose patron was Lord Cornwallis. The chief steward was my friend Stanley Calcutt, a big owner-grower and a conscientious member of the Hop Marketing Board. Unfortunately, as so often happens in England, the weather proved unhelpful and the competitors, some forty pairs, all from local firms, including Guinness, waited in a huge tent for the rain to stop. But it didn't and so they all tripped along to the Peacock Inn. A good example of the 'ill wind' proverb.

T.A. *Layton*, A Year at the Peacock, *Cassells, 1964*

Hop-Measuring Baskets

This anonymous letter, written in the form of a poem, describes a few of the hardships encountered by the itinerant families who travelled to Kent each summer for the hopping, and who felt they were being taken advantage of by greedy farmers. It also contains a veiled threat that the farmer should take heed of the message before the next year's workers arrive.

Dear sir, this letter I send
Knowing you to be the workman's true friend.
To this subject my mind has always been bent
Since the first day that I came hopping in Kent.

The farm that I work on has one hundred baskets or more
And the hops that we pick are dreadfully poor
To cheat us of our measure the tallyman's bent;
That's how we are treated when hopping in Kent.

When I went to school I was always told
That four pecks made a bushel, be it of sand or of gold;
But down here in Kent, how a measure to tell -
True: sure it would puzzle the devil from hell.

I measured our basket, and found it contained
Just eight bushels of the hops golden grain;
But our tallyman told us that that was meant
For a six-bushel basket when hopping in Kent.

Now, I think with Mr Simmons, I've a right to say
That the farmers would not like to be treated this way.
Yet self-preservation might make us intent
Upon doing as we are done by when hopping in Kent.
If a poor man steals a turnip, the farmer will feel
It is his duty to give him a month on the wheel;
They steal from us our labour, and we ought to be content
With any rough usage when hopping in Kent.

The huts that we sleep in, God knows, are well named;
They are "huts," not dwellings, and let in the rain;
They were not made for comfort. So pray be content
And never grumble at trifles when hopping in Kent.

Now, Mr Editor, to bed I must go.
For the embers of my fire are burnt rather low.
Next year when I come I hope to say with content-
They are forced to give us good measure when hopping in Kent.
The Kent and Sussex Times, *September 28th 1878*

Hopping in Kent

The hop that swings so lightly
The hop that shines so brightly
Shall still be cherished rightly
By all good men and true.
Thus spoke the jovial man of Kent
As through his golden hops he went
With sturdy limb and brow unbent
When autumn skies were blue.
Traditional Song

George Orwell goes Hop-picking

In 1931 George Orwell spent just under a month hop-picking at Home Farm, Wateringbury. He chose a bad year: the hops were poor and the weather worse, but this short extract from his account of the experience is a useful antidote to the 'hop that shines so brightly' view of hopping in the words of the previous song.

One day at hop-picking was very much like another. At about a quarter to six in the morning we crawled out of the straw, put on our coats and boots (we slept in everything else) and went out to get a fire going-rather a job this September, when it rained all the time. By half past six we had made tea and fried some bread for breakfast, and then we started off for work, with bacon sandwiches and a drum of cold tea for our dinner. If it didn't rain we were working pretty steadily till about one, and then we would start a fire between the vines, heat up our tea and knock off for half an hour. After that we were at it again till half past five, and by the time we had got home, cleaned the hop juice off our hands and had tea, it was already dark and we were dropping with sleep. A good many nights, though, we used to go out and steal apples. There was a big orchard nearby, and three or four of us used to rob it systematically, carrying a sack and getting half a hundredweight of apples at a time, besides several pounds of cobnuts. On Sundays we used to wash our shirts and socks in the stream, and sleep the rest of the day. As far as I remember I never undressed completely all the time we were down there, nor washed my teeth, and I only shaved twice a week. Between working and getting meals (and that meant fetching everlasting cans of water, struggling with wet faggots, frying in tin-lids, etc) one seemed to have not an instant to spare. I only read one book all the time I was down there, and that was a Buffalo Bill. Counting up what we spent I find that Ginger and I fed ourselves on about 5/- a week each, so it is not surprising that we were constantly short of tobacco and constantly hungry, in spite of the apples and what the others gave us. We seemed to be forever doing sums in farthings to find out whether we could afford another half ounce of shag or another two-pennorth of bacon. It wasn't a bad life, but what with standing all day, sleeping rough and getting my hands cut to bits, I felt a wreck at the end of it. It was humiliating to see that most of the people there looked on it as a holiday - in fact, it is because hopping is regarded as a holiday that the pickers will take such starvation wages. It gives one an insight into the lives of farm labourers, too, to realise that according to their standards hop-picking is hardly work at all.

One night a youth knocked at our door and said that he was a new picker and had been told to sleep in our hut. We let him in and fed him in the morning, after which he vanished. It appeared that he was not a picker at all, but a tramp, and that tramps often work this dodge in the hopping season, in order to get a kip under shelter. Another night a woman who was going home asked me to help her get her luggage to Wateringbury station. As she was leaving early they had paid her off at eight bushels a shilling, and her total earnings were only just enough to get herself and family home. I had to push a perambulator, with one eccentric wheel and loaded with huge packages, two and a half miles through the dark, followed by a retinue of yelling children. When we got to the station the last train was just coming in, and in rushing the pram across the level crossing I upset it. I shall never forget that moment-the train bearing down on us, and the porter and I chasing a tin chamberpot that was rolling up the track. On several nights Ginger tried to persuade me to come and rob the church with him, and he would have done it alone if I had not managed to get it into his head that suspicion was bound to fall on him, as a known criminal. He had robbed churches before, and he said, what surprised me, that there is generally something worth having in the Poorbox. We had one or two jolly nights, on Saturdays, sitting round a huge fire till midnight and roasting apples. One night, I remember, it came out that, of about fifteen people round the fire, everyone except myself had been in prison. There were uproarious scenes in the village on Saturdays, for the people who had money used to get well drunk, and it needed the police to get them out of the pub. I have no doubt the residents thought us a nasty vulgar lot, but I could not help feeling that it was rather good for a dull village to have this invasion of cockneys once a year.

George Orwell, The Collected Essays, Journalism and Letterts of George Orwell, Volume I, An Age Like This 1920-1940, *(1968).*

A *three part song*

I'm just in love with all these three,
The Weald and the Marsh and the Down countrie;
Now I don't know which I love the most,
The Weald or the Marsh or the white chalk coast!

I've buried my heart in a ferny hill,
'Twix' a liddle low shaw an'a great high gill.
On hop-bine yaller and wood smoke blue,
I reckon you'll keep her middling true.

I've loosed my mind for to out and run
On a Marsh that was old when Kings begun;
Oh Romney level and Brenzett reeds,
I reckon you know what my mind needs!

I've given my soul to the Southdown grass,
And sheep-bells tinkled where you pass,
Oh Firle and Ditchling an' sails at sea,
I reckon you keep my soul for me!
Rudyard Kipling, Puck of Pook's Hill, *1906*

6 · THE BIG HOUSE

Kent is a county of large houses – from the numerous medieval yeoman's halls to seventeenth and eighteenth century mansions. Its wealth is shown in the impressive number of stately piles whose owners benefited from the county's proximity both to London and the Channel coastline. Many of the great houses are open to the public, but the majority are known only to the student of architecture, or the genealogist, and glimpsed over tall walls or at the end of long tree-lined drives.

An Advertisement for a Cook

Required by a gent, near to Bromley in Kent,
A cook on plain cooking plainly intent.
She need not make entremets, sauces or jellies,
That cause indigestion and irritate bellies;
Enough if she's able to serve up a dinner
That won't make her master a dyspeptic grinner.
If asked to bake bread, no excuse she must utter;
Must be able to churn, and to make melted butter.
If these she can do - eke boil a potato,
And cook well a chop, with a sauce called tomato;
The writer won't care to apply further test,

That she's up to her work, and knows all the rest.
She must be honest, industrious, sober and clean,
Neat in her garb, not a highly dressed queen;
And must be content, whatever her age is,
With sugar and tea, and twenty pound wages.

Richard Pike, Remarkable Advertisements, *early nineteenth century*

Philip Sassoon in Kent

The greatest host of his day, the millionaire politician, socialite and art collector, Sir Philip Sassoon (1888-1939), lived in Kent at Port Lympne close to his Hythe constituency. The mansion was designed for him by Sir Herbert Baker, then involved in work at New Delhi. The estate is now home to a famous zoo park, its magnificent mansion taking second place to the wild animals in its grounds.

He was dressed in a red shirt open at the neck and velvet slippers embroidered with PS in gold, and looked exotically out of place in the wet Kentish landscape . . . In (Baker's) public buildings every proportion, every cornice, every piece of fenestration was . . . an object lesson in how not to do it. Port Lympne was no exception, and Philip's taste for interior decoration had not improved matters . . . Philip, more than almost anyone I have ever known except for Maurice Bowra and Vivien Leigh, had an idiosyncratic and infectious style . . . He saw the ridiculous side of Port Lympne. Going round the house we came on a particularly hideous bathroom, panelled in brown and black zig-zags of marble. Philip said, without altering the tone of his voice 'It takes you by the throat and shakes you.' The point of Port Lympne was the garden. Philip's extravagence, which was such an agreeable feature of his character, expressed itself in the deepest and longest of herbacious borders, the most colossal beds of blue delphinium, the most imposing staircases of yew hedges. He told us with great satisfaction that he had heard a guide taking round a party of visitors and saying 'All in the old-world style, but every bit of it sham'.

Kenneth Clark, Another Part of the Wood: A Self-Portrait, *John Murray, 1974*

Mrs Whatman's Housekeeping Book

The Whatman family were industrialists in eighteenth century Maidstone. Their money came from the paper industry and when Susanna Bosanquet married James Whatman in 1776 she moved into his newly-enlarged house next to his Turkey Court Mill on the edge of Mote Park. Seven years later they moved to a much grander house, Vinters, less than a mile to the north, where they could enjoy the profits of their trade away from the industrial buildings from which they derived. Susanna's Housekeeping Book was drawn up to make sure that the household ran smoothly and to ensure that the lady of the house was not bothered with trivial questions.

The Housekeeper washes and irons her own small things and her Mistress's. A board at Vinters has been put up for her in the mangling room, that the heat might be avoided in the summer.

Housekeeper mends her Master's silk stockings, ruffles his shirts, and new collars and risbands them. The maids have generally time enough to stitch them, if they are put in hand in good time.

The chambermaid's needle work is entirely under the direction of the Governess, as it is for the young ladies and for James, but she may be taken off whenever the Housekeeper requires her assistance below. As her house work is over so early in the morning, she has all the rest of the day to work at her needle, or assist in the house when much company or a busy time makes it necessary. She must rise to wash her own things with the other maids, and iron them of an evening.

All the linen looked over in the Storeroom Monday morning, and stains taken out, etc. Housekeeper to put any stitches in Mr Whatman's muslin neck cloths that Mrs W has not mended for him.

There should be a large table in the Storeroom for the maids to mend shirts or anything that requires pressing, for, although the Housekeeper sets out all this kind of work, yet unless it is tacked on upon a flat surface, it will seldom lay smooth, and occasions in the end more work by tearing out.

The Laundrymaid ought to stick a pin or make some other distinction upon anything that wants mending when she puts it in the basket, or if a string is wanted, etc. If any muslin goes to the wash with a large tear, it should be ruffed out.

To keep up the Bedchamber fires when fresh coals are put on, it is sufficient to press down the fire and throw the cinders up over the fresh coals, but not to stir up the fire first unless it is likely to be going out. A clear fire only requires pressing down. No fire should ever be put out with water. It makes the dust fly all over the room, and gives much trouble in cleaning the bars. The persons themselves are covered with blacks, and the cast iron back will be spoilt by cracking. This dirty trick of pouring water on the fire will also occasion the cast iron at the back of the grate to split.

All the servants may go to bed early, and some necessarily must, if they do their duty in the morning.

On Monday night the Housemaid need not sit up to warm the bed for her Master, as she is expected to rise very early the next morning to wash. The Housekeeper can do it while her Mistress is undressing.

The Housekeeper and Butler should see all fires and candles are out before they go to bed.

The first thing a Housekeeper should teach a new servant is to carry her candle upright. The next is those general directions that belong to her place in particular, such as not setting brooms and brushes where they will make a mark, and all those common directions.

A Housekeeper by practise must acquire so quick an eye that, if she comes occasionally into a room that is cleaning, she must see at once if it is going on properly.

One of the most useful common directions next to carrying a candle upright is that of putting away chairs, tables, or anything that goes next to a wall, with a hand behind it. For want of this trifling attention great pieces are frequently knocked out of the stucco, and the backs of chairs, if bending, leave a mark on the wall.

The beds always well shook.

If the under servants could be depended on for doing all their business according to the instructions that could be given them, the eye of the Housekeeper would not be necessary to keep everything going on in its proper way. But this is never to be expected, and as the mistress of a large family can neither afford the time, nor even have it in her power, to see what her servants are about, she must depend upon the Housekeeper to see all her orders enforced and every rule kept up. For rules are not laid down unnecessarily and, when neglected, the inconvenience is felt in future, tho perhaps not immediately, and when the mischief has crept in, it is too late to go back again to a preventive rule. At least experience proves it to be very difficult.

The Housekeeping Book of Susanna Whatman, *Geoffrey Bles, 1956*

Sonnet written at Penshurst in Autumn, 1788

Ye towers sublime! Deserted now and drear!
Ye woods! Deep sighing in the hollow blast,
The musing wanderer loves to linger near,
While history points to all your glories past:
And startling from their haunts the timid deer,
To trace the walks obscured by matted fern.
Which Waller's' soothing lyre were wont to hear
But where now clamours the discordant hern!
The spoiling hand of time may overturn
These lofty battlements, and quite deface
The fading canvass whence we love to learn
Sydney's keen look, and Sacharissa's grace:
But fame and beauty still defy decay,
Saved by the historic page - the poet's tender lay!

S. *Curran,* The Poems of Charlotte Smith, *Oxford University Press, 1993*

Ingress Abbey

Ingress Abbey almost became one of Kent's lost houses. Built in 1833 to replace an older house demolished when the site was earmarked for a Government Dockyard, it was always fighting against the tide of industrialisation along the Thames shoreline. In the twentieth century it became the Merchant Navy College and the house and park were both institutionalized. When the college moved out the house and grounds fell into a state of utter decay. Only recently has the mansion house been restored as a high quality headquarters building, and new housing in the park has provided the impetus to restore many of the follies and garden features which survive.

In this neighborhood is the beautiful seat of Henry Roebuck Esq., called Ingress, formerly Ince Grice. It occupies an elevated situation rising from the Thames, and commands a fine view of the river and opposite parts of Essex. This estate once belonged to the nuns of Dartford, and became vested in the crown at the Dissolution. Queen Elizabeth granted it out. It has since passed through various families, and was purchased, in 1788, by John Disney Roebuck Esq. Considerable improvements have, at different periods, been made by its possessors, both in the house and the grounds; the latter having been much enlarged, and adorned with plantations. In an elegant summer-house built in a cavity of the chalk cliffs, is a valuable collection of Roman altars brought from Italy, and arranged by the Earl of Bessborough, its then possessor, who also ornamented the gardens with statues, and other specimens of Roman sculpture. The grounds are uncommonly beautiful, and the house commands some delightful prospects.

James Dugdale, The New British Traveller, *London, 1819*

After making a brief survey of Mr. Harmer's Gothic Mansion, Ingress Abbey (built from the stone of Old London Bridge), from without the iron fence - that impassable barrier which skirts the grounds - we purpose winding round the hill to the left of the house, pausing awhile before the extensive view we obtain of the chalk pits beneath us, whose sides exhibit a precipitous surface nearly two hundred feet in height; above which may be seen towering a group of noble timber trees. Tram-roads connect these pits with the shore, along which are several wharfs, whence the chalk is being continually shipped off; and even the flints found amongst it have become a profitable article of commerce. Several thousand tons are used annually in the Staffordshire potteries.

The Pictorial Guide to Greenhithe, 1846

Somerhill, Tonbridge

Today an independent school, Somerhill near Tonbridge is an otherwise little-known Jacobean mansion to the south of Tonbridge. In 1880 Mary, Lady Monkswell visited it and wrote in her diary:

We went on Sat., 9 Oct to the Julian Goldsmid's at a splendid house, Somerhill, near Tonbridge. It looks more like a village than a house. We drove through a pompous park, up to a magnificent door, which was opened by many gorgeous footmen, who ushered us into the longest room (94 feet). Here we found the beautiful Lady Goldsmid looking like an angel in grey, & Sir Julian. The poor Goldsmids are much to be pitied. They have £100,000 a year & everything you can think of - except one, a son. This beautiful creature, who looks about 25, has had 8 children in 11 years, all girls. They are like a national school. The eldest is 11, the youngest 16 months, and Lady G. has vowed that there shall be no more. Their names are Violet, Edith, Marguerite, Beatrice, Maude, Theresa, Grace, Baby.

The only other visitors were a very old Mrs. Proctor, aged 80, widow of Barry Cornwall, the poet and mother of Miss Proctor who wrote poems; an uninteresting daughter & a gay young Italian-Englishman named Gaston Foa, with whom I made great friends & got on very well. I was quite pleased & encouraged to find that Sir Julian & Foa seemed to like talking and laughing with me. (My voice was pretty good; oh how thankful I am for that; it has been more or less bad since June.) It was a constant amusement to me to watch the lovely Virginia's (Lady G.) gowns. I can not understand how a poor thing, who has carried that most ungraceful burden 8 times, should not have forgotten all beauty of movement. Most women do, I observe. Like the Queen of Sheba, Lady G. showed me the schoolroom (into which Bob and Gaston made numerous uncalled-for visits), the nursery, her bedroom, dressing-room, cupboard lined with cedar, her lace - a point d'Alencon skirt- worth about £800 or £1000, her fans, 23 in all, till I had to remember that at home were Bino and Gerard, the two handsomest boys in the world.

On a visit four years later Lady Monkswell recalled

'We were lodged right away in the new wing next to the stables, together with the Count, M'Ivers & others; the cold was something arctic. It was about 90 yards from my room to the dining room. The dinner, & particularly the dinner table, was exquisite with rows of different coloured leaves. After dinner we went to the enormous drawing room upstairs, which is like the big room of a Venetian Palace. '

Mary Lady Monkswell, A Victorian Diarist, John Murray, 1944

Knole, Sevenoaks

Today Knole is one of the jewels in the National Trust's enviable crown of houses in south-east England. However, the protracted negotiations by which it came into their care, the Trust's decisions often overturned by the donor, Lord Sackville, and the shambolic opening arrangements are forgotten today by the thousands of visitors who come each year to see the largest private house in England. Here James Lees-Milne, instrumental in smoothing the transition of ownership from Lord Sackville to the National Trust, recalls the first painful opening season.

Over Easter 1947 there were 1,082 visitors and over the spring holidays a further 2,090. Mason was worried about the numbers, chiefly because of the bottle-neck passage up and down the great staircase (a problem which baffles and alarms the Trust today) and the deficiency of staff to cope. At times it was touch and go whether the three ladies whom Robin Fedden had engaged to look after the staterooms could manage until Mason himself took over control. In its eagerness to supplement the endowment funds the Trust was surely mistaken in over-encouraging visitors and over-publicizing the house. I waged a perennial battle against the publicity department whose interests were intrinsically the opposite of mine. And I managed to thwart their desire to stage an official handing-over ceremony. Lord Sackville was likewise dead against it. He did not see himself in the role of willing benefactor of the National Trust to be accorded grateful thanks on a public stage. He saw himself as the inheritor of a glorious palace the burden of which he had been forced by a disobliging new world to shift onto the shoulders of an alien organization while retaining, as far as it were possible, the status granted to him by the old world. A BBC Television unit filming Knole in May, and promising wide publicity, was in Mason's words to me adding salt to Lord Sackville's wounds. Yet Lord Sackville liked and praised our resident staff and appreciated Robin Fedden's tact and civilized demeanour. One of the three ladies, Barbara Tate, who had worked for Lord Sackville before 1939 and returned to Knole after war service to work there for the National Trust, retired only a year or two ago and lives in the house today.

On the whole the opening of Knole did not start off auspiciously. The geography of the rooms caused overcrowding, delays and irritations. The staff got worn out and somewhat browned off. Besides large numbers meant few tips for their pains. There were letters in Country Life complaining that crowds of people were being turned away. An old woman of 84 was knocked down by a car at the entrance. Did the National Trust have a comprehensive policy to cover it against further contingencies of the sort? Impatient visitors passed the time carving their names on the gatehouse door. Mrs Hugh Dalton, whom I accompanied to Knole more than once, considered quite rightly that special facilities should be provided for serious students of the works of art, and suggested a connoisseur's day. I agreed that we must arrange this as soon as we could.

Towards the end of the season I wrote to Robin: 'There must be something wrong at Knole. A great number of grumbles from visitors this year at having to wait hours and then ill manners of the wicket-gate people. When we (Mrs Dalton and I) were there everything seemed to work very smoothly, but I suspect that the dragoness at the gate, and that extremely gauleiter figure with a walking stick are probably extremely dictatorial with the public - at least they frightened us to death.' Robin agreed that 'the pre-Trust inhabitants of Knole still feel, and sometimes show, that they are doing the public a great favour in admitting them to My Lord's house at all.' This was unfortunately the attitude in evidence at Knole and some few other country houses where the Trust and the donor's staff worked both for the old master and the new. We learned from the experience that divided loyalties were regrettable and must somehow be prevented in future.

James Lees-Milne, People and Places, *John Murray, 1992*

Fox Hunting Dinner at Knole

When partying at Cobham, his Grace let it fall,
"Tell my friends I expect them at Knole's ancient hall,
To-morrow at seven; and this understand,
Let each bring a neighbour, or friend in his hand:
For we mean to be gay, and that time shall give place
To the sweets of the bottle, and charms of the chase."

Old Time heard the mandate, and pleas'd at the sound
The Duke's invitation flew speedily round:
The hall was lit up by the great chandelier,
And its panels adorn'd with the spoils of the deer;
Where the tale of Acteon was painted to life,
And the huntress Atalanta, Meleager's wife.

But above all the rest, to improve the design
The table was cover'd with excellent wine.
His Grace took the chair, as becoming a lord,
And these were the lads that sat down at his board:
Sir Horace below did duty in prime,
A better could not be selected by time.

Honest Honeywood came to partake of the sport,
And the Tildens were there from Old Ifield Court;
Next Dering, Sir Edward, the county's delight,
Who always stood up for the Kentish man's right;
Then Twisden, Sir Roger, a sportsman more bold
Ne'er cross'd o'er a saddle in heat or in cold.

Stout Boghurst was there, who had sat himself down
By Symmonds, Recorder of Rochester town;
And opposite Whiffle, a talkative elf.
Who always was telling strange things of himself;
'Squire Hoare, and young Stanhope from Chevening Place;
And these were the friends that surrounded his Grace.

Comport of the Castle, and old brewer Best,
Whose Butt has been famous from east to the west;
Bill Edmeads of Nutsted, and two or three more
The whole, in conjunction, might make up a score;
Beside a few stanch hounds, the best of the breed,
Which ever were famous for keeping the lead.

A bugle was sounded, the mirth to begin
When bounce went the corks, as the punch was brought in;
All forms of distinction were banished aside,
No thoughts on precedence, the offspring of pride.
All, all, was true friendship, that never beguiles
That springs from the heart enliven'd by smiles.

The Duke claim'd attention, all answered, "Hush! Hush!"
While he held up his bumper, and shew'd them the brush
This sentiment gave (the hall rang with sound)
"All jovial fox-hunters! Where'ere they're found."
Now round flew the toast, and to crown it with glee
We demanded the chorus of "three times told three."

Thus with high tales of sporting, the hunter's delight
And libations to Bacchus, we shorten'd the night;
The wine was so potent, the spirit so good
That to honour the Duke we took in a flood;
All, all was good humour, till young squire Hoare
Fell back in his chair, and could take no more.

Now merry Frank Mackwreth, a little anote
Emptied his glass down the young squire's throat;
This trifle excepted, our joys were complete;
And the bugle now sounds for the guests to retreat;
Upstanding, uncover'd, was claim'd from the host,
And fresh bumpers were fill'd for Sir Horace's toast.

"May health! peace! and plenty! still wait on his Grace,
With a son like himself, and no end to his race!"
Thus ended the meeting, and fox-hunters gay

Remounted their steeds and rode cheerful away.
Diana was up, for she knew they must roam
And kindly assisted in lighting them home.

The Sportsman's Vocal Cabinet, *early nineteenth century*

[*The Honeywood family lived at West Malling Abbey*
Isfield Court is near Gravesend].
The Dering family lived near Ashford,
The Twisdens lived at Roydon Hall, East Peckham.
Chevening is now the official residence of the Foreign Secretary.
The Comport family leased Cooling Castle, now the home of the pianist Jools
Holland.
The Best family, brewers of Chatham, still live in Kent as the Best-Shaw
Baronets.
The Edmeades family have lived at Nurstead Court for nearly five hundred
years.

Country House Visiting in 1759

In the eighteenth century it was common practice for well to do
travellers to gain admittance to country houses on presentation of
their card. Here visits are made to Mereworth Castle and Knole,
whilst other houses (Mr Master's - Yoke's Court) are mentioned in
passing, as well as a visit to High Rocks, still a popular tourist
destination two hundred and fifty years later.

Monday 21st May 1759
Breakfast at an Inn near Merriworth house, a Seat of Lord
Westmorland's being about 8 miles. No Conveniency for Lodging at
this Inn. Were greatly Entertained for 3 hours and more, with the
magnificence of the house and gardens; Saw the Shell Room, and
Birds, and the Egyptian piramid. And were entertained at his
Lordship's with a Cold Collation. One of his Grooms attended Them,
for a shorter Cut, thro' Esq. Masters grounds (which were extremely
pleasant) in their way to Tunbridge Town. No way in regard to the
Roads, could be worse than from Mr Master's. In Hadley Lane,
providential Escapes from Bone breaking. Refresht themselves at

Tunbridge Town, and reacht the Sussex Tavern at the Wells, which is 13 miles from Merriworth house to Dinner. Mr Lindo's family, the only persons at the Wells. In the Evening were upon the walks, and amused themselves in the Tunbridge Ware Shops. Visited the Mounts Ephraim, and Zion and Mount Pleasant and The Grove. About two Miles from this place thro' a most wretched Road for Carriages, you come to a place called the Rocks, which are of stupendous height, and romantick appearance.

Tuesday 22nd May 1759
Breakfast at Seven Oak which is 13 Miles, and saw the Duke of Dorset's house and park called Knolle. In the house are above 700 Rooms, the furniture almost as ancient as the house, but very Superb and grand. Infinite Numbers of pictures. A very fine one of the Ceremony of swearing in the Lord Warden of the Cinque Ports, the back View whereof is Dover Castle and the Country round; He has been Lord Warden upwards of 40 years. His Grace is so good natured and polite as to give an Assembly once a week to the Gentry residing near this place. One of the Grooms attended them on Horseback, to show the principal Views of the park. At this place is a good house belonging to one Esq. Lambert. Din'd at Bromley, and about 7 o'clock set out for London, Mr Goodwin taking his leave of the party, at the new Cross Turnpike, to go to Mortlake in Surrey,
On this Expedition the Ladies and Mr Mount occasionally rode their led Horses, and the Ladies to the great pleasure of the Gentlemen, Expressed the Satisfaction they had received throughout this Tour.
A Tour Into Kent, *1759, Berkshire Record Office, D/Emt F5*

7 · CHURCH AND CHAPEL

Our Christian heritage is greater than any other county. The county boasts two Anglican cathedrals – the two oldest cathedral foundations in England. Its parish churches dot the skyline and give character to its towns and villages. Kent's wealth based on wool and trade and industry was reflected in its church buildings which form such a rich inheritance.

The Arrival of Augustine

St Bede here recounts the arrival of Augustine and his followers to Kent, and the reception they received. The King of Kent, Ethelbert, was married to a Christian called Bertha who was already worshipping outside the walls of Canterbury in what we now know as St Martins Church. This account confirms the belief that it is the oldest church in England still in use.

Reassured by the encouragement of the blessed father Gregory, Augustine and his fellow-servants of Christ resumed their work in the word of God, and arrived in Britain. At this time the most powerful king there was Ethelbert, who reigned in Kent and whose domains extended northwards to the river Humber, which forms the boundary between the north and south Angles. To the east of Kent lies the large island of Thanet, which by English reckoning is six hundred hides in extent; it is separated from the mainland by a waterway about three furlongs broad called the Wantsum, which joins the sea at either end and is fordable only in two places. It was here that God's servant Augustine landed with companions, who are said to have been forty in number. At the direction of blessed Pope Gregory, they had brought interpreters from among the Franks, and they sent these to Ethelbert, saying that they came from Rome bearing very glad news, which certainty assured all who would receive it of eternal joy in Heaven and an everlasting kingdom with the living and true God. On receiving this message the King ordered them to remain in the island where they had landed, and gave directions that they were to be provided with all necessaries until he should decide what action to take. For he had already heard of the Christian religion, having a Christian wife of the Frankish royal house named Bertha, whom he had received from her parents on condition that she should have freedom to hold and practice her faith unhindered with Bishop Liudhard, whom they had sent as her helper in the faith.

After some days, the king came to the island and, sitting down in the open air, summoned Augustine and his companions to an audience. But he took precautions that they should not approach him in an house; for he held an ancient superstition that, if they were practisers of magical arts, they might have an opportunity to deceive and master him. But the monks were endowed with power from God, not from the Devil, and approached the king carrying a silver cross as their standard and the likeness of our Lord and Saviour painted on a board. First of all they offered prayer to God, singing a litany for the eternal salvation both of themselves and of those to whom and for whose sake they had come. And when, at the kings command, they had sat down and preached the word of life to the king and his court, the king said: 'Your words and promises are fair indeed; but they are new and uncertain, and I cannot accept them and abandon the age-old beliefs that I have held together with the whole English nation. But since you have travelled far, and I can see you are sincere in your desire to impart to us what you believe to be true and excellent, we will not harm you. We will receive you hospitably and take care to supply you with all that you need; nor will we forbid you to preach and win any people you can to your religion.' The king then granted them a dwelling in the city of Canterbury, which was the chief city of all his realm, and in accordance with his promise he allowed them provisions and did not withdraw their freedom to preach. Tradition says that as they approached the city, bearing the holy cross and the likeness of our great king and Lord Jesus Christ as was their custom, they sang in unison this litany: 'We pray Thee, O Lord in all Thy mercy, that Thy wrath and anger may be turned away from this city and from Thy holy house, for we are sinners. Alleluia.'

St Bede, Ecclesiastical History of the English People *(AD 731), Penguin Books, 1990*

A Cranbrook Custom

It is customary here when a newly-married couple leave the church to strew the pathway - not with flowers, but with emblems of the bridegroom's calling. For example, Carpenters walk on shavings; butchers on skins of slaughtered sheep; the followers of St Crispin are honoured with leather parings; paper-hangers with strips of paper; blacksmiths with old iron, etc, In other parishes in this county, however, butchers are favoured with 'Rough Music' made from marrow-bones and cleavers, and printers from 'Chases' (the technical term for the iron framework which encloses the types from which the impression in printing is obtained.)

The Archaeological Mine, c. 1860

The Fall of Wye Church Steeple

On Sunday, 21st March, 1686, after the conclusion of morning prayer, before all the people were out of the churchyard, the Steeple of the Parish Church of Wye fell, and beat down the greatest part of the East Chancel, and almost all of the South and North Chancels, together with one pillar of the Church; the ensuing year the Churchwardens put up boards at the east end of that part of the Chancel which continued standing, placed the Communion table there and railed it in; and likewise repaired the pews and other seats of the Church, together with the Pulpit, which had been damaged by the fall of the Steeple; and thus it continues to this day 1700.

Wye Churchwarden's Account Book, 1700

Court Cases in the Diocese of Canterbury 1559-1565

These cases show that family life in Elizabethan East Kent was every bit as complicated as the lives of some people in the twenty-first century. Church law covered many aspects of secular life as this selection shows:

Margaret wife of Thomas Lane is an eavesdropper and bearer of tales. She is a common slanderer and railer on the churchwardens and sidesman, saying they are procured knaves.

St Mary Northgate, Canterbury

William Blake after Evening Prayer fell out with the parson for speaking against great ruffs and breeches. He said the parson ought to speak only of parish matters and not of the Jews or the Pope. Though advised to revoke his words he refused to do so. He called the parson knave for declaring the Scriptures. He told the parson that he said more in the pulpit than any honest man would say.

Warehorne

William Clarke keeps ill rule in time of Service and drunkards in his house. He confessed that one Henry Fuller came to his house drunk on a Sunday in time of service, but he would not go when required to. The churchwardens appeared and said he had drunkards several times in his house.

St George, Canterbury

Widow Scudder went away with George Bakester of Brookland and has now returned. They confessed. He is to do penance on three Sundays in his own church and she in her own church any Sunday with bare feet until she is firm in her penitence.

Brenzett

Thomas Barton for incest with Agnes Garton when his servant and now living at Willesborough. He said that as his servant she slept in the same room as he and his wife. She called out in the night and, when they asked her the next day why she did so, she said that somebody lay on her. She told one Fox's wife that it was he. He denied.
Boughton Aluph

William Sharp of St Mary Northgate Canterbury married Helen Swetman of St Peter Canterbury and later married Elizabeth Tipping. He agreed that he had lived in adultery with Elizabeth Tipping and that he contracted marriage with Helen Swetman, banns published three times two years ago. He then married Elizabeth Tipping in the face of the church. He contracted with Rabage Nash about a fortnight before Christmas but banns were forbidden. The judge ordered that they were not to consort together, except in church or public places. He is to appear at the next sitting to show cause why he should not be excommunicated and to answer a charge of fornication with Margery Cheeseman. Later he was monished to produce Cheeseman a certificate of date and place of her death. Helen Swetman appeared and said she did not want to be in the case or to have the man.
St Mary Northgate, Canterbury

Henry Cleygate of Headcorn, being asked if he could help anything by witchcraft, confessed that, praying by the help of a god, he could. He learnt it of his mother about sixteen years ago, also of Sir Thomas Saunders, priest of Sutton, ten or eleven years ago. He was declared convicted. Did not appear. Excommunicated.
Headcorn

Alexander Grigesbye does not go to his own parish church on Sundays, but goes to Linton. He admitted it and was monished to go to his parish church of Loose henceforth under pain of the penalty provided by statute. Dismissed.
Loose

Roger Swetman has been absent from church for six Sundays. He is dead.
Deal
Extracts from A J Willis, Church Life in Kent, *Phillimore, 1975*

For the new spire: Wingham Church

In seventeen hundred and ninety three,
Richard Hodgman, of Folkestone, he coppered me,
And fixed on my head a magnificent Vane,
Which discovers the way of the wind by the same.
'Twas the fifth day of August this work was begun
With intent for to keep me from rain, wind and sun,
But some seem to think that never would be done.
This matter by many had oft been discussed,
Which was the best covering and which was the worst;
Some were partial to copper and some for lead,
And others said shingle will serve in its stead,
But I on that point will never trouble my head,
If you finish me well, for to make me secure,
So that I a hundred of year may endure.
Anonymous, 1793

Canterbury Cathedral

Pride of old Kent; thy venerable walls
Thy storied windows, rich with many a dye,
Through which the varied day-beam dimly falls,
Thy gorgeous shrines, and towers that brave the sky,
Long shall attract the stranger's wandering eye,
Though now no pilgrim bends o'er Becket's tomb,
Though Dunstans's ashes all unhonoured lie,
Though now no longer pious hands illumes
The lamp o'er Anselm's grave, gilding the midnight gloom!
Arthur Brooke, 1818

Canterbury Cathedral

In the centre of the louvre or lantern of the Bell Harry Tower is a
circular aperture, closed by a wooden trap-door. In the Chamber above
there is, or there was, a windlass for drawing up rolls of lead or other

materials for repairing the higher parts of the tower or of the roof of the Cathedral. One of the workmen in the employ of the Church was deaf. He, on one occasion when the windlass was to be put in operation, was stationed in the upper chamber, and when the work-men below brought in any load, and had fastened it, they pulled the rope as a signal and he began to turn. Mr Simmons, vestryman, predecessor of Thomas Wright, was in Beckets or the Upper Chapel, when looking westward he saw a boy holding the rope rise above the organ. Thinking this some boyish folly yet terrified for the consequences, he hastened thro' the Choir. He was in terror when he saw the boy nearly at the top and then saw him rapidly let down. He did come down in safety without falling, but with hands dreadfully lacerated and almost lifeless with pain and terror. It appeared that this boy, a King's Scholar, coming in at the south door, which was open for the workmen who were unloading their lead and material outside, saw the rope pendant and taking hold of it and pulling it, the man above began to draw him up. The poor boy thought it was fun and that he would only draw him a few yards and then let him down. However he soon found that he was being gradually drawn up, and so held as tightly as he could. When the deaf man, at length saw him, instead of landing him, he immediately in fear for the boy began to wind the rope back and to let him down. This rendered the danger double. He came however down without a fall. I have tried in vane to discover the boy's name.

So too, I could not find out the name of another King's Scholar who was locked into the Cathedral, and supposed that he must continue there all night. At the time the Organ stood in the north aisle of the Choir.... The boy ensconced himself under the steps leading to the organ loft when it had grown dark. About 9 o'clock however, Dr Buckworth, whose house opened on the terrace by the north door, being in want of a book from the library, entered the Church by that north door with his lantern and proceeded to the library. The light as he passed cast its ray down the passage from the Library door across the North Transept. The boy saw the glimmer, was affrighted and screamed out. The Doctor was surprised but advanced to discover whence the screams could proceed, found the alarmed boy, took him to his House, gave him refreshment, afterwards noticed and patronized him thro' life.

The Reminiscences of the Revd George Gilbert (1796-1874), 1938

Cobbett visits Tenterden

The agriculturalist William Cobbett made a progress across Kent in 1823, and whilst his main interest was in observing the ways in which the land was used, his comments on other aspects of rural life are of interest too. Here he cannot resist commenting on the parish church of St Mildred, Tenterden which he found filled with box pews, reflecting the social status of the inhabitants of the town.

The church at this place is a very large and fine old building. The tower stands on a base thirty feet square. Like the church at Goudhurst, it will hold three thousand people. And, let it be observed, that, when these churches were built, people had not yet thought of cramming them with pews, as a stable is filled with stalls. Those who built these churches had no idea that worshipping God meant going to sit to hear a man talk out what he called preaching. By worship they meant very different things; and, above all things when they had made a fine and noble building, they did not dream of disfiguring the inside of it by filling its floor with large and deep boxes made of deal boards. In short, the floor was the place for the worshippers to stand or to kneel; and there was no distinction; no high place and no low place; all were on a level before God at any rate. Some were not stuck into pews lined with green or red cloth, while others were crammed into corners to stand erect, or sit on the floor. These odious distinctions are of Protestant origin and growth. This lazy lolling in pews we owe to what is called the Reformation. A place filled with benches and boxes looks like an eating or drinking place; but certainly not like a place of worship.

William Cobbett, Rural Rides, *J. M. Dent and Sons Ltd. 1912*

Nonconformity

Nonconformity was an early starter in Kent, and by the mid nineteenth century, a period of relaxed religious toleration, there were some rather unusual sects in existence. The Walworth Jumpers, the Peculiar People and the Agapemone all claimed adherents in the county, but the sect to cap them all, the Jezreelites, was based in

Gillingham. Remembered long after the sect's demise by their huge uncompleted temple, they had strange forms of worship which included 'open services' where children were allowed to preach. A local newspaper report shows how astonishing these events must have been.

The service in Israel's Hall, Napier Road, was largely attended on Sunday afternoon, when the proceedings were conducted by three little girls. Emma Petry, aged thirteen, of Stratford, took for her subject 'The one widow, one leper, one hundred-fold, or 144,000 living bones'. 'The Mariner's Chart across the Trackless Ocean' was the subject on which Georgina Watson, aged twelve years, of Kilmarnock, Ayrshire, addressed the congregation; and Janet Watson, aged fourteen, also of Kilmarnock, spoke on 'Why Christendom seeks Life through Death'. The whole of the subjects were well treated, and were listened to with much pleasure. One of the most important features in the service was the excellence of the singing, which was led by a piano, six harps, four violins and a piccolo.

Chatham and Rochester Observer, *May 17th 1884*

A Home in Kent : an epitaph

Mine be a home on some sweet Kentish hill,
Screened by ancestral oaks from winter's chill,
Where the first golden rays of sunrise stream
And sunset brightens with its latest beam!
Blest with a rich variety of view, -
The calm clear river, all in silvery sheen,
Running with noiseless motion through the vale;
The church in sight, with ever verdant yew,
And lichen-gate with ivy ever green.
Ye happy homesteads and broad orchards, hail!
The cheerful windmill, and the fields of corn,
And fragrant hop with aromatic scent!
Here would I live, and die where I was born,
On some sequestered hill in lovely Kent.

Benjamin Gough, Kentish Lyrics, *1867*

From the Ightham Churchwarden's Account Books

Until the nineteenth century, the officers of the Parish Church fulfilled many functions now carried out by the Civil Authorities. A Parish rate was raised each year to cover these expenses, and these extracts from the accounts give a hint of the variety of the payments.

1708   Paid for a badger's head 1s. 0d.

1730   Paid for one poule Catt 6d.

1772   Paid the Borsholder Expence in Detaining Two men at the George for a fraud 19s. 4d.

1775   Paid the Hanoverian Doctor for cureing George Comber as per agreement £2. 2s. 0d.

1780   Relief to Crazy Mary 5s. 0d.

1781   Paid for Repr Wd Caryer's Spinning Wheel 1s. 0d.
Paid Mr Knight's bill for Eating, Drinking and Detaining Thos. Stone 2. 18s. 7d.

1783   Paid for cutting 14 thousand of Turf at 4 Shillings pr Thousand £2. 16s 0d.
Paid Dame Hubbard and two Old Men 11d.

1786   Paid one pound of Mutton for Dame Marshall 4d.
Paid Mrs Collings for Spining half a doz of 7d thread 3s 6d
Paid Mr Wells for the Wrotham Turnpike £3. 0s   0d.

1788   Memorandum by a Vestry held this Day it is agreed that Dave Sanders should be allowed one Shilling per week for his child being a Nidget.

1789   Gave the old men for Tobacco 6d.
Paid Thomas Nash for shaving the Old Men at the workhouse 28 weeks 10s 6d.

1791   Give Jno Hollons to Get a Drink for his Child being bitt by a Mad Dog 15s. 0d.

1793   Paid for Labour in Parson's Lane £2. 5s. 10d.

1795   Paid John Glover of the Parish of Wrotham for four People sent to the Pest-House with the Small Pox, 5 weeks at 12 shillings per week each £12. 0s. 0d.

1797   Paid Mrs Parris for Schooling for the Workhouse Children and Books for one   9s. 9d.

1798   To a New Pair of Hand Cuffs   2s. 10d.

8 · KENT AT WORK

Long before what we call the Industrial Revolution of the late eighteenth century, Kent was an industrial county. Its raw materials included wool, fruit timber, ragstone, flint and coal. Power was provided by water and wind. The process of industrialisation started when the Romans extracted iron ore in the county; later, medieval masons quarried and carved; breweries sprang up wherever there was a pure water supply; papermakers established themselves at Dartford in the seventeenth century whilst all around the coast and up the rivers fishermen and boat-builders found a livelihood. It must always have been a noisy county – with only the more remote downland being entirely free from the industry which brought prosperity, and which continues to do so to this day.

The Shrimp Industry

Gravesend has ever been noted for its shrimp industry, more particularly in earlier days when hosts of visitors spent their annual holidays here. For the purpose of shrimping, which is still carried on successfully by local merchants, the bawley boat is used, the cost per boat in the old days being about £200, and each was manned by two men. Up to a few years ago some 100 men were engaged in catching shrimps, and they resided for the most part in East-street and West-street, their homes being models of cleanliness and order. The boats rarely go beyond Southend, and they work at all times of the day and night; September being the busiest time of the year. What is called a 'Trim-Tram' is used for catching the shrimp, but the Leigh-on-Sea fishermen use the 'Death-Trap.' Each boat has a galvanised copper and boiler on board, everything being kept spotlessly clean. Some two gallons of water are placed in the copper and in about two minutes it is boiling. There are two kinds of shrimps - one brown and the other pink, the former being a specie of lobster and the latter a specie of prawn. The record catch of a Gravesend bawley boat is 120 gallons in a haul. Shrimps will never remain where bad or impure water exists, proving the cleanliness of the fish, which form a very popular dish on the tea table. The Gravesend shrimp still enjoys the reputation of being superior to any other caught around the coast.

F.A. Mansfield, The History of Gravesend, *The Gravesend and Dartford Reporter, 1922*

Coal in Kent

Friday 25th August 1989 is a date that will be remembered by not only the 630 men employed at Betteshanger Colliery, but also by those who had been employed there over the previous 60 years. The closure of the colliery also ended the existence of the Kent coalfield.

In the 1930s men travelled from all over the United Kingdom to this new colliery which was owned by Messrs Pearson and Dorman Long Ltd. Many men did not have the fare to travel by bus or train and so walked to Deal and the surrounding district to find work. On arrival at Deal they were not made too welcome by the local inhabitants, who were rather concerned about the mass influx of 'foreigners' into this seaside town and farming area.

After the housing estates had been built at Betteshanger Colliery village and Mill Hill in Deal it was said that there was an invisible barrier at the bottom of Mill Hill, above which was not looked upon as part of Deal. It must be said that whilst some of the newcomers were rather rough and ready, the majority with their families wanted to settle in their new environment, and mix with the locals. Some grocer's shops displayed the sign 'Miner's Bacon', where were the cheap cuts, but as time went on the traders realised that the workers at Betteshanger Colliery had a considerable bearing on the increase in their takings.

The number of employees increased to nearly 3,000 and the colliery had a very good customer in the Southern Railway as the coal produced was excellent steam raising coal. It also supplied the domestic market locally.

As the colliery was the one closest to France it was bombed a number of times during the war. Although there was an anti-aircraft gun site at the end of the colliery tip, the German fighter bombers used to fly very low across the English Channel, undetected by radar, drop their bombs and quickly return to their bases in France. On one occasion part of the colliery boiler house and fan house were destroyed and several men lost their lives. This caused a problem for the men working underground as they could not be brought to the surface as the winding engines were steam driven. The men had to wait underground for several hours before an emergency winder could be erected which brought the men to the surface a few at a time, a very lengthy process. One bomb dropped just outside the lamproom, making a big cloud of black dust and a very large hole, but luckily it never exploded. On examination it was found to be full of nuts and bolts, thanks to some foreign worker in a German factory.

After the war working conditions at the colliery were poor. Coal was produced by pick and shovel and the ventilation was very bad. Men emptied their boots when they became full of sweat. Wages were on piecework and men were paid on results. If geological conditions were poor then wages were low and men had to make their money when conditions were good. At this time many coal faces were affected by water and at times the men were working in water up to their knees and sometimes above.

In 1947 the coal industry was nationalised and after some time conditions of work did begin to improve and much money was spent on dust suppression underground as many men suffered from silicosis or pneumoconiosis, the scourge of all miners.

Later the first miner to elected as a councillor on the Deal Borough Council was Billy Marshall, a real character, who could be seen every Sunday on Deal seafront speaking on his 'soapbox'. The miners were being recognised as inhabitants of the town of Deal at last.

As time progressed mechanisation was slowly introduced

underground and the pick and shovel method of working gradually began to disappear, although some types of work could not be mechanised. Men had to be trained in this new method of working and the younger element found it easier than the older ones.

Over the years the colliery had its 'ups and downs' and geological conditions in Kent were not as good as some other coalfields in Great Britain. In 1969 Chislet Colliery was the first to be closed. Tilmanstone Colliery followed in 1987. A large number of miners took either voluntary retirement or voluntary redundancy or were transferred to other collieries. In 20 years the Kent coalfield had gone from four collieries to none.

East Kent Within Living Memory, *Countryside Books, 1995*

A Medway Delicacy

Smelts are small fish of the Salmon family, and like their more famous relatives swim long distances to spawn. They were a particularly Kentish delicacy until the 1940s when they suddenly disappeared from the Medway. A doble is an eighteen foot long clinker-built fishing boat.

Smelts first appeared in the Medway estuary each year in August when they could be found in small numbers in Sharfleet and Half Acre creeks. From August to February they graduallly came up as far as Chatham and Rochester. Cockham Wood Reach, 'Brickie' (opposite Gun Wharf, Chatham), Limehouse Reach and Tower Reach were good places, both in winter and at the end of the spring spawning when the smelts were on their way downriver again, 'The Slack' at Gashouse Point - almost opposite Strood Pier - was another favourite place which could be worked only during the last hour or two before high water. In this place, contrary to the usual practice, the net was rowed round against the direction of the tide in the mainstream, while avoiding the barge blocks off Acorn Wharf. These winter smelting places at Rochester and Chatham, being close to the homes of the fishermen, were heavily fished when the smelts arrived. The men assembled in their boats, often several hours before the appropriate time, to book their places in the queue. This was called 'laying-in', the late-comers could be relied upon to encourage the ones at the head of the queue to make a start. As one crew were hauling in their net, another doble was curving a second net round and sometimes the smelts filled up the vacuum so quickly that many crews would get a good haul, although the lucky ones would have got their net down at exactly the right time to scoop the best catch. Sometimes a crew, arriving at the spot to see the tail-enders making poor catches, would wait, laying-in to try their luck when the tide turned and the net could be worked from the other direction.

It was traditional knowledge that in places upriver of Wouldham, smelts could only be caught at night, there being one exception: Halling Hole. At Wouldham and Horne's Place, Cuxton, they could be taken both in daylight and darkness and below Horne's Place only during daylight hours. Slack water is necessary for using the drag-net and above Rochester all the smelting places had to be worked in the last hour or two before low water. First the dobles had to be rowed and poled upriver for a mile or two so that they could be worked back downstream on the last of the ebb, making perhaps four or five hauls in the traditional places where a bend in the river, a gravel bank or even an outfall pipe caused slack water where the smelts were known to gather. Every smelt 'shoot' had its own name, passed down by word of mouth from father to son and from master to apprentice and often these fishermen's names are not those marked on maps.

Derek Coombe, The Bawleyman, *Pennant Books, 1979*

Cloth in Cranbrook

It was Edward III who conceived the idea of participating in the material benefits enjoyed by the Low Countries from this commerce, and he resolved to increase the manufacture of cloth in England. His queen was Phillippa, daughter of the Count of Hainault, titular overlord of the Netherlands, and Edward had personal experience of the prosperity of Flanders and the immense wealth of her merchants. In 1331 he granted passports to several clothiers authorising them to travel from Ghent to England with their men and servants for the purpose of 'working wool and exercising their mystery.' Strict injunctions were issued to ensure to the newcomers a good reception, and penalties were threatened to any who should hinder or molest them.

The privileges and benefits granted to the newcomers were extended to the home weavers and clothworkers, who were encouraged to adopt the new methods introduced from Flanders. The government wished to concentrate the industry in selected towns and counties, a different type of cloth being manufactured in each district. London and Norwich, cities with an established trade in cloth, The Cotswolds, Somerset, Yorkshire, Essex, Suffolk and Kent were the chief places decided upon, and in Kent the location most suitable for the production of broadcloth was Cranbrook.

With the introduction of water power for the fulling mills and the use of marl as a cleansing agent, the reason for the choice of Cranbrook as a centre for making cloth becomes apparent. Standing in the midst of a countryside watered by many small brooks, running in narrow valleys easily dammed to regulate the water power; with the mighty oaks of the Forest of Andred to furnish timber for the mills and a plentiful supply of marl available, all the necessary requirements were readily at hand.

With cloth making firmly established, a period of great activity commenced in Cranbrook and the neighbourhood, for the industry rapidly extended to the surrounding villages of the Weald. This first phase rose to its maximum effort towards the end of the fifteenth century and continued, with little falling off for nearly another century. There were setbacks such as occurred in 1528 when trade with Flanders was interrupted as a result of the foreign policy of Henry VIII and Wolsey. This occasioned great hardship to all classes. Sir Henry Guldeford in a report to the Cardinal asserts that 'the clothiers of Kent had so little sale of their cloth that many would be idle in the county.' London merchants refused to buy cloth brought to them by the cloth makers, and there was unemployment of spinners, carders, weavers, and other craftsmen. The weavers of Cranbrook and the Seven Hundreds petitioned the Council to enforce the Statute passed in the reign of Edward IV ordering clothiers to pay the wages of their artificers in ready money. In an effort to relieve the situation the Cardinal summoned a meeting of the London merchants, and commanded them to buy their cloths as heretofore under pain of the King's high displeasure.

In the Weald there was general discontent, and a plot was discovered for the overthrow of Wolsey. It was planned to capture him and get him to the coast, where a boat in which holes had previously been bored was ready to take him to sea. The leaders claimed the support of many weavers and clothworkers of Cranbrook and Goudhurst, and Frittenden pledged one hundred men to aid the project.

After the fall of Wolsey and the re-establishment of our markets abroad, the industry quickly regained its prosperity. The annual production in Cranbrook and the Weald at this time was estimated at 12,000 pieces. Early cloths made in Kent had a length between 30 and 34 yards, and weighed 66lbs., but an act passed in the reign of Edward VI ordered that 'every piece of broadcloth that should be made in the Shire of Kent must contain in length, when thoroughly wet, between 28 and 30 yards, in breadth one three quarter yards at least, and when thicked, scoured, milled and fully dried, should weigh 84lbs at the least.' Much of the output from the looms of Cranbrook was exported to Flanders, in a partly finished state, or not 'barbed and shorne' these processes of teasing and shearing being done there. The finished cloths were then despatched from Antwerp to all parts of the world.

C.C.R.Pile, Cranbrook Broadcloths and the Clothiers, *Cranbrook and District Local History Society, n.d.*

9 · MILITARY MATTERS

With its long coastline and proximity to the continent, Kent has known military occupation for thousands of years. Much of the Battle of Britain was fought in the skies over Kent. Where would the Medway Towns, or Dover or Folkestone, be without the military? Even in times of peace they give financial stability to the area, provide a focus and add character. As this selection shows, they are often involved in things that would – at first glance – seem outside their remit. Long may they form part of the Kentish landscape.

The Henrician Castles

Kent was heavily defended in the sixteenth century against an invasion by Spain, and castles were newly built at Sandown, Deal, Walmer and Sandgate. They were all based on a bastion design where the gun emplacements were designed to fire over emplacements at a lower level. Many were constructed using strong brick vaulting, and some incorporated stone from recently closed monastic property.

King Henry the Eight (whose care, and coste, for the defensing of this Realme against forreine invasion, is rightly comparable with any thing that either Eadgar, or Alfred (Kings before the Conquest), bestowed, and merely incomparable with all that ever any other his predecessors have attempted) did at the same time, and for the same respect, that wee have opened in Dele before, defraie £5000 and above, upon this platfourme, which lieth within the parish of Folkestone toward Hythe, and hee called it (of the sandie place where it is pitched) Sandgate castle.

William Lambarde, A Perambulation of Kent, *1576*

Mary de Medici visits Canterbury

In 1641 Henry Oxinden, a member of a long established Kent family, wrote to his brother about the stay of Mary de Medici in Canterbury.

I give you thanks for the newes you send mee: here is little. The Queene mother arrived at Dover about 7 of the clocke upon Saturday night: she made some stay agt. Sir Tho. Wilford's Welke woods where shee had some fruit which came from my brother Bargrave's presented unto her; I saw her take a peare, and her 2 dogs drinke some water, but somewhat disdainfulle in regard the glase where the water was in was not brought upon a silver plate, which was much inquired for.

The Queene mother did not unmaske, but in requittal of some few ladys' and gent. attendance there did vouch safe to have the bate of the Caroch put downe and threw her vest upon it, where they and myself had the honour (if it may bee called an honour) to salute the hem thereof there was the lord of Arundell and the lord of Oxforde and some few others with her.

The Thursday before, Sir Tho. Palmer, Sir George Theobald, my Cosen Oxinden and myself waited upon the lady Oxinden and my Cozin Oxinden's lady to the king's pallace at Canterbury where she lay: after dinner about 3 of the Clocke wee were admitted into her presence: after the ceremony aforesaid she did my Cousin Oxinden's lady the honour as to speake to her, who answered her in soe good French as shee was commended for it, and this was esteemed noe small favor.

British Library, Add. Mss 28,000 f.356
[The woods at Ileden, where the Queen's dogs refused to drink from bowls that had not been brought on a silver tray may still be seen off the A2 south of Canterbury; the Royal Palace had been created amongst the remains of St Augustine's Abbey just outside Canterbury's City Walls.]

The preparedness of Kent for a Spanish Invasion, 1587

It seems from this report that the county was well prepared for the possibility of an invasion by sea in the years leading up to the Spanish Armada. Its author, Lord Cobham, was the last of his family to play a major role in county life, after more than two hundred years of faithful service.

There are trained in this county 2,500 men and put under captains; to which His Lordship hath added 700 more with the good liking of the county. 300 horse put in readiness under captains; to each captain 50, with a lieutenant, trumpet, cornet and all in suitable cassocks. There are appointed to each company of 300 trained men, 50 pioneers; and to every company of 200 men, 39 pioneers furnished under the leading of the head constables of the place where they are levied, and to every companie two carts. The Justices will see 300 shot mounted upon ordinarie naggs for the firing of the beacons, viz. 50 out of each lath. The Justices quorum and th'other Justices have agreed to find petronells but such of them as have the leading either of horse or foot desired to be eased thereof, in respect they are otherwise employed.

Lord Cobham, Report to the Privy Council, *quoted in* Archaeologia Cantiana, *LXXXV*

A Balloon Flight from Dover Castle, 1785

This, the first cross-Channel balloon ride, took two and a half hours, and ended with Mr Blanchard landing safely at Guines, having virtually stripped naked to avoid ditching at sea. The next day he was offered the Freedom of the town of Calais: later, a Rowlandson engraving was published to celebrate the event.

On Friday January 7th, the wind being NNW very moderate, and the sky clear, Mr Blanchard, accompanied by Dr Jefferies, took his departure for the Continent, in his balloon, from the Castle at Dover. Three guns were fired from the castle at nine in the morning, and the flag was hoisted upon the firing of the first gun, as a signal that the Aeronauts were preparing to fill the balloon. About ten minutes before its ascension, a fourth gun was fired, as a signal that they were about to depart. The balloon was completely filled by one o'clock; the vessel which ascended with it, in the five former voyages, was affixed; the intrepid voyagers took their seats; the oars and fly used in the last voyage were placed in the boat. Nine bags of ballast, the French Edition of Mr Blanchard's 'Voyage with Mr Sheldon'; a large inflated bladder, containing a number of letters from people of the first distinction in this country, to several of the French Nobility; a compass, and some philosophical instruments; a small bottle of brandy, two beautiful silk ensigns, English and French; a few biskets, and two cork-jackets, made the whole of their cargo. Mr Blanchard had adapted an apparatus to sustain himself and friends, without the boat, which weighed 64 pounds, if they should have occasion for an addition of levity upon the voyage. The balloon was filled in about two hours and a half, and the process conducted by Mr Blanchard and Mr Decker, of Berwick-Street, Soho. They ascended at thirteen minutes past one, close to the large gun well known by the name of Queen Anne's Pocket Pistol. Mr Blanchard kept the balloon in exact equilibrium for a considerable time. The greatest silence reigned among the numerous concourse of spectators, until Mr Blanchard had got so far from the cliff, as to be over the Sea; he then stood erect in the car, and saluted the spectators most gracefully, by bowing, taking off his hat, and waving his ensign. He was then cheered with the loudest acclamations.

The Execution of Stephen Fox, 1857

Executed on August 20th 1857 for the murder of his sweetheart.

So lonely in my cell I sit,
Alas! I am compelled to die,
I ofttimes weep with tears of sorrow
That I might not see the coming morrow.

Poor Anne! Thou art dead and gone,
For thee, poor soul, I ofttimes mourn,
My sentence is not too severe,
For I murdered her I loved most dear.

How oft I've walked our minds to ease,
Beneath the Dane John's shaded trees,
Sweet tales of love we oft did tell:
To my native City I say farewell, farewell!

Lamentation

Come all you men and maidens, and listen here awhile,
I courted a lovely maiden, her heart I did beguile,
I worshipped poor Ann Hadly; my heart with grief doth flow,
I curse the day, likewise the hour, I proved her overthrow.

For six months I her courted, I loved the girl so dear,
I feared she loved another, and I proved too severe,
I promised I would marry her; at last she did me scorn,
I cursed the day, and the hour that e'er I had been born.

Many an hour we wandered on, over beauteous hill and dale,
When I think on happy hours I have cause to bewail;
To see her with another live, I think my heart would break,
I die upon the gallows tree for Ann Hadley's sake.

We went unto the house of God, it makes my heart to bleed,
To think that I premeditated this cruel, wretched deed;
I hired a pair of pistols, I meant this deadly strife,
I sold my soul to misery, and took away her life.

My time is fast approaching, I think it hard to die,
Dark visions now appear to me; I do for mercy cry;
No mercy did I show to her, I deeply feel the rod,
Her soul I sent so unprepared, to appear before her God.

Alas! Poor Ann Hadley, her life time was but short,
Her blood in torrents it did flow by pistol's sharp report;
Your bleeding form is before my eyes - alas! I soon must die,
And I must seek forgiveness from the great God on high.

I shudder at the moment that I am called to go,
I've lost all I loved on earth, she proved my overthrow;
God pardon me for what I've done, I hope to be forgiven,
O pardon for a murderer, and receive his soul in Heaven.

You lovers all, these lines you hear, take warning by my fate,
Govern all your passions, before it is too late,
Intemperance and bad company has brought me to this doom,
It will soon be over, I bid farewell, though dreadful is this gloom.
Stephen Fox, in a script sent to his printers, Mather and Co., Whitechapel,
1857.

Chatham in the Eighteenth Century

Not a flattering description of this Naval town, but one which was
probably nearer the mark than many of its residents would have
publicly acknowledged. Even Dickens, nearly a century later in
Pickwick Papers *described Chatham as 'The productions of these*
towns appear to be soldiers, sailors, Jews, chalk, shrimps, officers and
dock-yard men.'

Of all the spots on Britain's shore,
Examine every country o'er,
Sure ne'er was seen the like before,
    The well-known town of Chatham.

Fair truth directs my honest muse,
Here drunken sailors and ships crews,
Whores, Baptists, Methodists and Jews
    Swarm ev'ry part of Chatham.

Possess'd of ev'ry female grace,
Of shape, and air, and blooming face,
By Nature made for Love's embrace,
    Are fam'd the Girls of Chatham.

Whene'er inclin'd to am'rous play,
The wanton God points out the way,
Then who so kind, and fond as they?
    Ask all the Bucks of Chatham.

Great shade of Hoyle, assist my quill,
To tell how much thy dear Quadrille,

Is eager sought Old Time to kill,
   In every house of Chatham.

Such raptures rushing through each breast,
Whene'er a Pool the Gamester's blest,
'What pity Sunday's made for rest!'
   Exclaim the Belles of Chatham.

Proud Rochester and Strood may talk,
Of pavements smooth, and roads of chalk,
For those who chuse to ride or walk
   Not so the folks of Chatham.

Contented in their dirty hole
They hobble on with meaner soul,
Contriving how to save the cole,
   Who would not live at Chatham?
The Kentish Gazette, *November 19th 1771*

Coastal Defences

Some Kent coastal defences are here described through the eyes of an early nineteenth century visitor. The Martello Tower was one of a chain of early nineteenth century coastal defences built to counter a perceived French invasion. The shaft which was visited at Dover is now known as The Grand Shaft and connected the harbour and cliff top on the western side of Dover. It is now open to the public in summer, and is is regarded as one of the outstanding feats of early nineteenth century engineering.

20th Sept 1823 We went into a Martello Tower of which there are a great many all round the coast, wherever there is a weak place that an enemy might attack. These are generally inhabited by the preventive service which is called the coast blockade, but the one we went into was held by a pensioner. There are no guns up all round the coast, the wall is 7 feet thick, there are 3 different floors in it, the lowest a coal hole, the next above it is a magazine and the third a dwelling. The gun is fixed on a pivot on the top landing and is turned round to a point. Dinner at 3 - then we all walked up hill by the church to go to Saltwood Castle. Uncle and Aunt stopt and we went in to the Castle which is a fine ruin belonging to Mr Croft and inhabited by a farmer.

23rd Sept 1823 Walked with Mama and Aunt (Papa and Uncle went to call on Mr Stride) through the streets home, then had a donkey chaise and went up to the castle, which consists of a grand keep with a square tower at each corner. It is surrounded with a yard, barracks among which is the governor's house, and a walk, then a deep foss over which is a draw bridge and an outer wall. An old warder shewed us over the castle - there were no guns mounted - all the magazines were full - only 7 soldiers there now. We saw the old keys of the castle and an old Roman sword of state and 2 Elizabeth pocket Pistol 8 ins. Long, and part of the old towers and walls of Hubert de Berg. From the cliff a fine view of the town and the coast of France - there are there piles of canon balls and shells. When we came down I walked with Papa to look at the shaft which is a winding staircase, round a well with windows looking into it, reaching from the top to the bottom of the cliff.

The Diary of Charles Powell, Centre for Kentish Studies U934 F8

The Battle of Britain

The author H.E. Bates, today most famous for writing The Darling Buds of May, *lived in Kent. Here in his autobiography he describes Kent at the time of* The Battle of Britain.

The Battle that presently began in that torturingly beautiful summer will always be known as the Battle of Britain. Of its supreme importance I will say more in a moment. But geographically, of course, it covered no more than a tiny fraction of Britain. The area of combat took place in a cube roughly eighty miles long, nearly forty broad and five to six miles high. The vortex of all this was Maidstone, Canterbury, Ashford, Dover, Dungeness area, in which Spitfires largely operated, with the further rear centre of combat between Tunbridge Wells, Maidstone and London, largely commanded by

Hurricanes. Sometimes in the frontal area as many as 150 to 200 individual combats would take place in the space of half and hour.

To the civilian population below, who were able to see something of a battle for the possession of their island for the first time in centuries, the entire affair was strangely, uncannily, weirdly unreal. The housewife with her shopping basket, the farm labourer herding home his cows, the shepherd with his flock, the farmer turning his hay: all of them, going about their daily tasks, could look up and see, far far above them, little silver moths apparently playing against the sun in a game not unlike a celestial ballet. Now and then a splutter of machine-gun fire cracked the heavens open, leaving ominous silence behind. Now and then a parachute opened and fell lazily, like a white upturned convolvulus flower, through the blue midsummer sky. But for the most part it all had a remoteness so unreal that the spectator over and over again wondered if it was taking place at all. Nor was it often possible to detect if the falling convolvulus flower contained an enemy or a friend, and often the same was true of aircraft: so that the battle was watched in the strangest state of suspense, with little open or vocal jubilation.

It was of course, with its combatants, much glamorised by newspapers; but Richard Hillary was right when he said 'much that is untrue and misleading has been written on the pilot of this era. Within one short year he has become the nation's hero and the attempt to live up to this false conception bores him . . . The pilot is of a race of men who since time immemorial have been inarticulate; who, through their daily contact with death, have realised, often enough unconsciously, certain fundamental things. It is only in the air that the pilot can grasp that feeling, that flash of knowledge, of insight, that matures him beyond his years.' This was just as true of the far less glamourised bomber pilots, as I was later to discover.

Remote though it may have seemed to the spectator below there can however be no shadow of doubt that the Battle of Britain was the most decisive of the war. Its closest parallel is Trafalgar. Both were the beginning and not the end of the long road to victory. A good many years were to elapse between Trafalgar and Waterloo; another five of bitter and extensive combat on air, sea and land were to elapse between mid-September 1940 and the surrender of the German armies at Luneberg Heath in 1945. This book offers no space in which to argue over the inter-allied conflicts and duplicity that went on in those years, bitter though their results may now seem to the British mind; it simply remains to say that if the Luftwaffe had knocked out the R.A.F. in that unbearably beautiful summer of 1940 it is scarcely possible that we would have hoped to achieve another Waterloo.

Throughout it all I wrote little. It was a world in which you felt there was no tomorrow. You lived for the day; and the day, you hoped, by the grace of God, would be enfolded mercifully by a night in which men didn't kill each other. The nights, as I remember them, were of a marvellous starlit calm; the days broke limpid and soft and flowered into a perfection that mocked and pained by its beauty. Like an old hen protecting its brood I hovered protectively about my young family, holding it to be my duty, for the present, to see that they at least had a protective umbrella held above them. They, after the manner of children, grew to accept it all more readily than their parents, so that there came a day when a great blast of thunder broke out above the house and all of us dived under the kitchen table, the children weeping with fear until pacified by their parent's soothing words; 'There's nothing to worry about. It isn't thunder. Only bombs,' so that tears were silent and dried in a moment or two.

As the summer drew on, growing always in beauty, until once again the wheat was the colour of brandy in the fields, it became clearer and clearer that the climax of the battle was still to come. You felt your nerves begin to stretch to breaking point. Not only did it presently seem as if there were no tomorrows; there were no todays either.

At this moment, Madge's brother paid us a week-end visit. Far away in Northamptonshire he had been as remote from battle as a nurse in Kensington Gardens might have been from Sevastopol or Khartoum. He found it impossible to believe that war was being raged above his head. I don't think he slept well; but in the morning he came forth with a marvellously sensible suggestion. We would go fishing. I myself hadn't fished for years and neither of us had a hook or line to our name. Accordingly we went out and spent some magnificent sum, about two pounds I imagine, on the two cheapest rods we could find, hooks, lines, floats and shot. We dug vast quantities of worms and mixed great puddings of paste. We then armed ourselves with beer, cheese and sandwiches and set off finally for the two pretty little lakes that lie in the centre of the village, one of them containing an island

of quince trees, with the limpid narrow River Stour running alongside
them by woods of alder and hazel and here and there under big old
horse chestnuts and half drowned ancient willows.

An immense peace enshrouded us; in a garden an old man placed
an even older ladder against an apple tree glowing with early red fruit
as with lanterns; a kingfisher streaked, copper and blue, through the
dark tunnel of alders; a flight of mallards winged away above the
quince trees; moorhens dived and disappeared and pranced their
delicate way among the tall thick summer reeds. It was hard to believe
that this was a battle-field. The paradox of war and the ethereal
exquisite nature of summer dissolved together to form a sort of opiate,
a state where time and its senseless, fragmentary paroxysms of pain
and fear no longer existed. We simply were; we sat beside the still
waters; and there was nothing else that mattered.

The little river hadn't been fished for years and as we cast in our
lines it was like taking chocolate from innocent and unprotected
children. Fat perch and roach, sometimes a small pike, an occasional
rudd or silver bream; all came to see us as if we were hypnotists. Even
in the heat of the day we went on hauling them in. Then suddenly the
opiate heat of noon was shattered. A dog fight broke out above us
with such unexpected suddenness that I thought at first it was the
boughs of the big tall poplars catching noisy fire above our heads.
Machine-gun shells spattered down the full centre of the lake, rousing
a thousand fish, big and small, from August slumber, so that they
leapt out of the water in silver frightened shoals as if pursued by some
monstrous legendary pike. We angled with a little more
circumspection after that, seeking the shelter of trees; but though we
heard once or twice again the rattle of machine-gun fire there was
really nothing that could destroy the suspended beauty of that day,
which had calmed at least one troubled mind and given it hope for the
future.

The immediate future was in fact to be one of blackness. With the
coming of September the Germans were to make another full and
deliberate attempt to destroy Britain. The full premeditated nature of
the attack, based on Goering's personal orders from France, was clear:
it was to smash London and with it, if possible, the entire morale of
the people. The first attack, on September 7th, was the heaviest the
country had ever had to face. Very heavy bombers, Dornier 215s,

were used, escorted by powerful fighters, including the new Heinkel 113. The Luftwaffe bomber force, outnumbering the R.A.F. many times over, was over London for hours, commanding the sky. Docks, stores, warehouses, masses of working-class houses and buildings of all kinds were smashed. By night, from fifty miles away, we could see from our Kentish fields the great red-orange light of London burning. Throughout it all the outnumbered R.A.F. fought like tigers and though in the heat of battle it is never easy to assess casualties with any accuracy we claimed to have shot down a hundred Nazi planes. Against this over 300 Londoners were dead and another 1600 injured.

This was by no means the end. On September 15th a new great mass of bombers with their fighter escorts was again pitched against us, London again the main target. In one of these desperate moments when something has to be done to hide fear from children and distract them from a catastrophe about to blow up in their faces we had trundled off, pram, kettle, food, fishing rods and all, to picnic by the lake. The quinces were already turning gold on the trees by the water and the day was as golden as the ripening fruit. We had scarcely begun to fish when the sky, from the south-east, the direction of Dover, began to blacken. It was darkened all over by what seemed to be a monstrous gathering of giant starlings. Helplessly we watched them, at no height at all, flying above our heads, in relentless formation, on their way to London. As they passed there was suddenly, among the reeds on the lake, an explosion, followed by another. Though by no means loud, it frightened us more than the bombers, even long after we had discovered that it had been caused by two addled wild-duck eggs bursting in the summer heat.

Again a small, ludicrous event, remembered after nearly thirty years, illuminates an affair of far more sinister import. In the recollection of the exploding duck-eggs lies the thought, tenuous but satisfactory, that that day, September 15th, was virtually the end of Goering's effort to destroy us. Fat duck-egg as he himself looked, it was he, not us, who was that day exploded. We claimed - again, probably in the heat of battle, mistakenly - 185 Nazi planes destroyed. The precise number hardly mattered to a dozen one way or the other. On the 18th, 27th and 30th we claimed a further 230 and after that the Luftwaffe fire was virtually expended.

Those who lived in the south-east that summer will never forget the irony of its ethereal beauty and its deathly, deathless conflict. When the weather broke at last, bringing autumn rain, it also brought an odd, repeated phenomenon. I have never seen it before and I have never seen it since.

It was a sun-dog: a kind of evanescent circular rainbow that, in unsettled weather, appears just a little away from the perimeter of the sun. It had about it a kind of ominous beauty. It might almost have been a sign from heaven: a portent, but of what you were too tired or shattered or relieved to wonder.

H.E. Bates, The Blossoming World, *Michael Joseph, 1971*

Prisoners at Tonbridge

The writer and politician Harold Nicolson lived at Sissinghurst Castle, where he and his wife Vita Sackville-West created the famous gardens. Here he describes seeing German prisoners during the Battle of Britain.

7th September, 1940

At Tonbridge, where we change trains, there are two German prisoners. Tiny little boys of 16 they are, handcuffed together and guarded by three soldiers with fixed bayonets. They shuffle along sadly, one being without his boots, shuffling in thick grey socks. One of them just looks broken down and saturnine; the other has a superior half-smile on his face, as if thinking, 'My Fuhrer will pay them out for this.' The people on the platform are extraordinarily decent. They just glance at them and then turn their heads away, not wishing to stare.

The sirens yell and we get into our train for Staplehurst. At Sissinghurst, we have tea and watch the Germans coming over in wave after wave. There is some fighting above our heads and we hear one or two aeroplanes zoom downwards. They flash like silver gnats above us in the air. The all-clear sounds at 6, but there is another warning at 8 which actually lasts till 5.30 am., but I go to sleep.

Harold Nicolson, Diaries and Letters *1939-1945, 1967*

Take Cover

I was born in London in 1911 and in the autumn of 1914 I caught diphtheria and was very ill. On recovery I should have gone to a convalescent home but these were needed for wounded soldiers, so I was sent to stay with my aunt and uncle in Rainham in Kent.

My uncle kept a jewellery shop in the High Street. He also sold gramophones, records and mouth organs, which were very popular with the soldiers as they were small enough to put in their pockets and take back to the trenches. The parish church of St. Margaret's was on the opposite side of the road and had a lovely peal of bells. There was a row of horse chestnut trees in front of the church. On Sundays in spring, people from Chatham and Gillingham came on the open top tram to admire the blossom and get a breath of air.

My uncle's shop was between the bank and the post office. Next to the post office was the vicarage. Once a year there was a garden fete in the vicarage grounds. My aunt helped with the strawberry teas and uncle ran the bowling games. I loved the donkey rides. In the evening there was a concert in the vicarage drawing-room. It was a very jolly affair.

A very large sign at the entrance to Rainham read 'Motorists must not exceed 8 miles an hour through the village'. Of course, a great part of the traffic was horse-drawn vans and carts and bicycles during the war years. One Saturday morning I was playing in the garden when I saw some planes coming over. The black crosses on them were plain to see as they were flying low. I rushed in to tell my aunt that German planes were coming over. She did not believe me until she came to check as the air raids had always been at night. The planes were on their way for the first daylight raids on London. We had numerous raids and heard heavy gun fire, sometimes a plane was shot down. My uncle was medically unfit for the army but, when a raid was coming, he had to cycle round the outlying villages crying 'Take cover' and when it was all over return and shout 'All clear'. He had a connecting bell from his bedroom to the post office next door which received the first warning.

West Kent within living memory, *Countryside Books*, *1995*

The Great Review at Woolwich

This extract from a street ballard commemorates the celebrations held at Woolwich following the Coronation of Queen Victoria in 1838, and contrives to send Her Majesty on an imaginary pub-crawl of the garrison's most popular taverns!

For miles around fam'd Woolwich Town
One moment give attention,
And of this glorious grand review,
A word or two I'll mention,
See thousands flock from far and near
All ranks from every quarter,
With coaches fine the roads are lin'd,
and ships upon the water,

See kings and foreign princes too,
Who came our Queen to crown sir,
All come to see the grand review
This day near Woolwich Town sir;
See Marshall Soult that soldier brave
Who with Bonaparte had dealery,
Sent over by the King of France
to view our bold artillery.

As I went over Plumstead Common
I met a man, oh ! fegs sir;
He was a Greenwich Collegeman
Upon two wooden legs sir;
By cannon balls his legs he lost
He said in battle handy,
And he'd meet the Queen at 6 o'clock
all at the Marquis of Granby.

A blooming lass in Union Street
Said England's Queen had told her
She'd ramble over Woolwich Town
When she'd review the soldiers;
She would call in at the Woodman first
Then ride towards the water

And call in at the Fortune of War
And then the Royal Mortar.

Then at the Duchess of Wellington
Awhile she'd take her station,
Down Powis Street and Hare Street
And back to the Salutation,
And then to view the Arsenal
Some said the Queen would go sir,
Then call in at the Prince of Wales
and visit the Three Daws sir.

Then right along through Woolwich Town
Where folks would at her gaze hard
And sing God save our maiden Queen
As she pass'd by the Dock Yard,
The ladies at the White Horse
And the Blue Anchor stationed
Will shout so keen, God Save the Queen
We have seen the Coronation.

A lady came three hundred miles
Because somebody told her,
When she got round to Woolwich Town
They would take her for a soldier;
And when she found she wouldn't do
To grief she did resort to
And at one jump went all the way
From there to Tilbury Fort sir.

So fill your glass and let it pass
This day to Woolwich Town sir,
It is just a week this very day
Since England's Queen was crowned sir.
Long may she reign and happy be
And live in peace contented
And ease the woes of everyone
Who has for years lamented.

10 · PEOPLE

What is an area without its people? Old and young, rich and poor, it is the people that give Kent her character. What they build, and how they choose to do it, are but visual signs of mankind's own requirements, beliefs and influences. Kent is no different to any other county in this respect, but the following selection will give a small insight into some of the more unusual characters from the county's past.

Gravestone of a Greenwich Landlady

Assign'd by Providence to rule a tap,
My days passed glibly till an awkward rap,
Someway, like bankruptcy, impelled me down,
But I got up again and shook my gown
In gameson gambols, quite as brisk as ever,
Blythe as the lark, and gay as sunny weather;
Composed with creditors, at five in pound,
And frolick'd on till laid beneath this ground,
The debt of Nature must, you know, be paid,
No trust from her - God grant extent in aid.

The Appetite of Nicholas Wood

In 1604 Nicholas Wood, of Harison, Yeoman, eat a whole sheep of 16 shillings price, raw, at one meal; another time he eat 30 dozen of pigeons; at Sir William Sidly's he eat as much as 30 men; at the L. Wooton's, in Kent, he eat at one meal 84 Rabbits, enough for 168 Men allowing each half a Rabbit; he devoured 18 yards of Black Pudding, and having eat 60 pounds of cherries, said that they were but wish Meat; he eat a whole Hog at once, and after it, three Pecks of Damsons, and this after Breakfast, for he had eat a Pottle of Milk, a Pottle of Pottage, with Bread, Butter, and Cheese, before. He eat in my presence, saith Taylor, the Water Poet, six penny wheaten Loaves, three sixpenny Veal Pies, one pound of sweet Batter, one good dish of Thornback, and a shiver of a peck Loaf an inch thick, all in an hour; the House yielded no more so he went away unsatisfied; yet John Dale was too hard for him at Lenham, who laid a wager that he could fill Wood's Belly with wholesome victuals for two Shillings, and a Gentleman added that when he had eaten up Dale's two shillings he should perfectly eat up a whole Sirloin of Beef. Dale brought six pots of Mighty Ale, and 12 new penny white Loaves, which he sopped therein, the powerful fumes whereof conquered the Conqueror and laid him asleep, to the preservation of the roast beef and unexpected winning of the Wager. He spent all his estate to provide for his Belly, and tho' a landed man, died poor about the year 1630.

Crouch's Admirable Curiosities, 1718

A Witch in West Langdon

November 28th 1762. A number of people surrounded the house of John Pritchers, of West Langdon, in Kent, and, under a notion of her bewitching one Ladd, a boy of 13 years old, dragged out his wife by violence, and compelled her to go to the said Ladd's father's house, about a mile from her own, where they forced her to go into the room where the boy was, scratched her arms and face in a most cruel manner to draw blood, as they said, of the witch, and then threatened to swim her; but some people of condition interposing, the poor woman's life was happily preserved, and the persons concerned in carrying out the imposture, particularly one Beard, and Ladd's wife being carried before a magistrate and compelled to make satisfaction to the unhappy injured woman, the mob dispersed, and the country, that was everywhere in tumult, is again quieted. The boy pretended to void needles and pins from his body, and his father and mother upheld the deceit, and collected large sums of money on those whose compassion was excited by so melancholy a situation.

The Annual Register, Kent, *Vol. 5, 1762*

Joseph Conrad in Kent

The author Joseph Conrad lived in Kent from 1909 until his death in 1924. Firstly in a cottage in Aldington, then at Capel House, Orlestone. The family then moved again to a house at Wye – which turned out to be haunted – before finally taking up residence at Oswalds in Bishopsbourne, between Canterbury and Dover. The valley possesses a 'Nailbourne' or intermittent river which rises and falls from year to year, and which forms the object of many local legends and rumours. Here John Conrad describes an incident involving his father, and the Nailbourne.

One day after returning from Canterbury my father stamped his foot, which he often did when something was not to his liking. Luckily he was by a chair which he grabbed as the floor-boards broke and fell into the space below. When we had recovered from our surprise we noticed that there was the sound of flowing water coming from below the floor. There was a strong smell of fungus and rotten wood, and after pulling up some more flooring we could see that the water was coming in through the brickwork below the front door cill, trickling under the joists and disappearing through the foundation brickwork opposite. Temporary repairs were made until a new floor could be laid during which time we should have to go away. The stream through the garden began to dry up and so did the water under the floor. No one had any explanation for this underground stream; the owners were not interested, merely saying that it would be attended to with any other work that needed doing. I went along to the forge and discussed it with Milward, who told me that the stream that flowed along behind the forge and through the garden of Oswalds, had originally flowed along the side of the village street through the gateway to Oswalds and on under the front door, hall and passage and into the lake at Bourne Park. Sometime in the eighteenth century the stream had been moved over to its present position but whoever diverted it did not know or had ignored the fact that there was and still is an underground stream flowing beneath the visible 'Nailbourne'.

John Conrad, Joseph Conrad: Times Remembered, *Cambridge University Press,* *1981*

Formerly to be seen in Gillingham Churchyard

Sacred
To the Memory of
THOMAS JACKSON, Comedian.
Who was engaged 21st of December, 1741, to play comic cast of characters, in this great theatre - the world; for many of which he Was prompted by nature to excel.

The season being ended, his benefit over, the charges all paid, and his account closed, he made his exit in the tragedy of Death, on the 17th March, 1798, in full assurance of being called once more to rehearsal; where he hopes to find his forfeits all cleared, his cast of parts bettered, and his situation made agreeable, by Him who paid the great stock-debt, for the love He bore to performers in General.

The Visit of Elizabeth I to Dover

In 1573 Queen Elizabeth made a progress through Kent. She stayed at Westenhanger for a night and on resuming her journey to Dover she was met at Folkestone Down by the Mayor and Jurats who presented their compliments to her. But they were somewhat eclipsed by the arrival of the Archbishop of Canterbury, the Lord Cobham and a huge number of knights who accompanied her to Dover where she stayed a week. In 1587 Elizabeth came again, this time to see that the coastal defences were sound, and also to see whether the Cinque Ports really deserved their special privileges. She announced 'she did not meane to suffer them in such fruitless manner to enjoye so great privileges without doing any service, but to resume them into Her Majestie's hands and to reduce them to the same terms that the rest of her subjects bordering upon the sea coast are in'. She was in no favourable mood when she came, but perhaps she thought it wiser, in view of the national emergency, to do nothing about curtailing the privileges of the Cinque Ports

C.H.Bishop, Folkestone - the history of a town, *Headley Brothers, 1973*

Edith Nesbit in Kent

The novelist Edith Nesbit, author of The Borrowers *and* The Railway Children, *had many Kentish associations. She is buried in the churchyard at St Mary in the Marsh, close to her holiday home, but her main residence for 23 years was Well Hall at Eltham, a magical house that has since been demolished. The bangles mentioned in the following extract were a gift from her husband, each one representing a new book. The following is an account of the high-life at Well Hall.*

The Bland's parties were large and frequent, and played an important part in their lives. Many notabilities attended them. Often ten or more of us would band together for the tiresome journey from town to join the seven or eight inhabitants of the house for an evening's amusement which was usually kept up until the small hours. It seemed a long and tedious way to go, and on a foggy night, after waiting perhaps an hour for a train at Cannon Street, and then being shot out to wait again on the chilly platform at Blackheath to catch the Well Hall train, one wondered why on earth one had accepted one's invitation so readily.

One arrived late without a qualm (for meals were invariably late there) to be greeted by a large placard at the principal entrance saying briefly "The Front Door is at the Back!". This was because the front door opened directly into the long hall where we dined when there were a lot of us, and it was therefore undesirable to let in the cold air. Or the notice might imply that there was more chance of being let in at the back; with any luck a gardener's boy, a child, or even a maid might hear us. Generally, even when we had made our entrance the prospect of dinner seemed to be remote, and we wandered about feeling forlorn and neglected, and still wondering why we had come. Mrs Bland would be finishing a chapter, and Hubert his article for the Chronicle, and we knew that nothing could happen until their work was done.

Then at last Mrs Bland would appear on the stairway, radiant - in riotous spirits, perhaps, because she had just escaped premature death by not falling over a dustpan left on the stairs; and that was, of course, an omen that it would be a good party. She always wore the same kind of dress, a long flowery silk one, probably with Turkish slippers, and certainly with many silver bangles. These reached nearly to her elbow and were never removed. They were presents and she prized them as an Indian prizes his scalps. She bathed in them, and they got in her way often, but I never saw her freckled arms without them until I went down to Romney Marsh at the very last, and she showed me that her hands were so thin that she could slip them off easily.

Her companion, Miss Hoatson, wore the same flowing dresses, but hers had more form about them, and a waist line. Hubert would at last crawl lazily out of his 'den' in "immaculate evening dress" with velvet coat and a monocle worn on a black watered-silk ribbon which hinted at foppishness, though the glass was a necessity.

The dinners themselves were always "chancy". If poems, articles, and books were going well, they were quite grand. At one time two Swiss lads did the cooking, and were full of surprises. I remember once they made little chalets of white sugar with real lights inside as a sweet. In leaner times we had a huge soup-tureen of haricot beans doled out graciously and gaily, without comment by Madame, a large block of cheese to follow, and delicious apples from the garden. There was always plenty of red and white wine in beautiful Venetian bottles and the table looked lovely. Hubert had passion and skill as a rose grower. In the summer we (the guests) used to gather a wicker clothes-basket full of roses, picking them off short to save the remaining buds. We would make a thick mat of them from one end of the long table to another, setting in at intervals the silver branch candle-sticks that Mrs Bland adored.

The party never flagged once the Blands had appeared. A friendly atmosphere hung about them, an atmosphere of festivity. They were intensely lovable; and we were gay because we knew that our hostess was enjoying the large company, and thinking how lucky she was to have got so many "darlings" together. The conversation was good, and everyone was given a chance to express his own ideas. Hubert was a brilliant talker, but he was also eager to listen, especially to youth. "Remember the respect due to youth" was one of his favourite sayings. Edith herself would wind on for hours if she was in the mood, while the children of the house were never shut away, and gave their opinions as definitely and dogmatically as the rest of us.

Invariably in the midst of the most distinguished gathering, one would find some weak or wounded creature who was taking shelter at Well Hall - a baby rescued from poverty or illness (who surprisingly appeared at late dinner), a poor relation waiting for a job, a painter seeking recognition, a timid girl whom someone there believed in and encouraged to write stories. No one who knew the Blands could resist seeking their comfort and their counsels in distress.

After dinner we danced in the cleared drawing-room, and there were games and more talk. Devil-in-the-dark caused the destruction of so much good furniture all over the house that it had to be stopped. Mrs Bland collected old glass lustres long before there was a craze for them, and there were fine chandeliers in the drawing-room, which contained many beautiful pieces.

The dinner and dancing and talk lasted so long that most of us missed last trains and slept where we could, the men usually finding accommodation in the garden cottages. Next morning it was considered in the best taste to depart by an early train without seeing our hosts. The house would be in an incredible muddle, and the most tactful procedure was to breakfast with Paul, the eldest son, who left early for the City, and then vanish unheeded.

Doris Langley Moore, E. Nesbit, *Ernest Benn, 1967*

Courtship in Dartford

A cook-servant, having received a letter from a young man, some distance from Dartford, with proposals of marriage, and being incapable of reading and writing, requested her fellow-servant to read it for her, which, of course, occasioned much laughter for some days. Betty had seen the young man, and liked him, but did not like a third person to know her reply; she, therefore, got a blank letter directed to him, and enclosed a match. The young man readily comprehended her meaning, re-visited her, and soon after they were married at Dartford church.

Mockett's Journal, *1824*

Thomas Arden of Faversham

One of the earliest plays of its kind, Arden of Faversham *was by an unknown playwright in the time of Marlowe and Shakespeare and told the story of the murder of Thomas Arden, one time Mayor of Faversham. It was, in effect, the dramatisation of a tale that had already been widely reported and talked about. Arden was murdered on his wife Alice's orders so as to allow her to cavort with her lover Mosby. A farcical chain of events eventually led to Arden's death in a house that now bears his name in the town, and the subsequent execution or horrible deaths of all those involved. This extract tells of his wife's first, unsuccessful, attempt to murder her husband.*

There was a painter dwelling in Faversham who had skill of poisons, as was reported. She therefore demanded of him whether it were true that he had such skill in that feat or not, and he denied not but that he had indeed. 'Yes' said she 'but I would need have such a one made as should have most vehement and speedy operation to dispatch the eater thereof.' 'That can I do' quoth he, and forthwith made her such a one, and willed her to put it into the bottom of a porringer and then after to pour milk on it; which circumstance she forgetting, did clean contrary, putting in the milk first, and afterward the poison. Now Master Arden, purposing that day to ride to Canterbury, his wife brought him his breakfast, which was wont to be milk and butter. He, having received a spoonfull or two of the milk, misliked the taste and colour thereof, and said to his wife, 'Mistress Alice, what milk have you given me here?' Wherewithal she tilted it over her hand, saying, ' I ween nothing can please you.' Then he took horse and rode to Canterbury, and by the way fell into extreme purging upwards and downwards, and so escaped for that time.

Holinshed's Chronicles of England, Scotland and Ireland, *2nd edition, 1587*

Sir William Courtenay

In May 1838 the last battle fought on English mainland soil took place outside Canterbury. The self-styled Sir William Courtenay, a Cornishman who had stood for the parliamentary seat of Canterbury in 1832 on the back of the Reform Movement, and who had subsequently been admitted to a lunatic asylum raised a rebellion which, though swiftly put down, resulted in his own death as well as in those of nine others. Seven of the deceased were buried in the churchyard at Hernhill where a memorial marks the event. The 'Rebellion' made national news, and ghoulish tourists immediately descended on the scene of the incident at Bossenden Wood. The Maidstone Journal of 1st June 1838 described the scene.

By far the most horrible spectacle was at the Red Lion (at Dunkirk). Here in a stable, ranged with their heads under the mangers, lay the bodies of Courtenay and six of his miserable dupes. At the moment of entering, the horrors of the scene were aggravated by a young woman having fainted, who, being severely pressed by the crowd outside, had for relief been admitted within. Immediately on beholding the frightful scene she sank senseless on the ground, her hands falling on the bloody garments of one of the dead rioters, and for a long period it seemed doubtful if animation would ever be restored. Yet many other females were outside, eagerly pressing forward to gain admittance!

Maidstone Journal, *1st June 1838*

The Times *then continues the story:*

On Sunday night the crowd of applicants for admission to the Red Lion was so numerous, and their conduct was so violent, that the landlord was compelled to close his doors and windows, and nail them fast, to prevent the irruption of strangers into his premises. There were apprehensions at one time that there would be a riot, and information of those apprehensions was forwarded to the magistrates; but fortunately peace and order were restored, and their interference became unnecessary.

The Times, *6th June 1838*

In Crayford Churchyard

Here lies the body of Peter Isnell, thirty years clerk of this parish: he lived respected, a pious and mirthful man, and died on his way to Church to assist at a wedding, on the 31st August 1811, aged 70 years. The inhabitants of Crayford raised this stone to his cheerful memory, and as a tribute to his faithful service.

The life of this clerk was just threescore and ten,
During half of which time he had sung out Amen.
He married when young, like other young men;
His wife died one day, so he chaunted Amen.
A second he took, she departed, - what then?
He married, and buried a third with Amen.
Thus his joys and his sorrows were treble, but then
His voice was deep bass, as he chaunted Amen.
On the horn he could blow as well as most men.
But his horn was exalted in blowing Amen.
He lost all his wind after threescore and ten
And here with three wives he waits till again
The trumpet shall rouse him to sing out Amen.

Siegfried Sassoon in Kent

The great First World War writer lived in west Kent, and this extract from a recent biography describes the house in Brenchley bought by his parents.

In *The Times* on 23 April 1884, an advertisement appeared for the sale of a residence known as Weirleigh, Brenchley, Kent. Theresa and Alfred had decided that they would live in the country but within convenient reach of London. Alfred boarded the train at Charing Cross for Paddock Wood, from where he made a short journey and gained his first view of the house above whose door was emblazoned in Latin: Vero nihil verius - Nothing is truer than truth. Built in the

1860s, Weirleigh stands at the point where the road from the village of Matfield takes a sharp incline to Paddock Wood and the railway station. This strange pile of Victorian architecture had previously been the home of the nature artist and cat lover Harrison Weir. He had an obsession for adding to the house, with the result that it lacks symmetry. Theresa was critical of Harrison Weir's architectural ideas, which she constantly attacked as wasting so much space. None the less the house enveloped her and for the next sixty years was the centre of her life. Of Weirleigh and its garden the adult Siegfried wrote, 'it is the background to all my dreams both pleasant and unpleasant.' Wandering through the rooms for the first time is like revisting familiar surroundings, so accurate and vibrant are Siegried's descriptions of them. This is especially true of the square, light-oak staircase which rises past the room where he and his brothers were born. As one stands at the top and looks down the well of the staircase, the spirit of place which he evokes in *The Old Century* and in his poetry, is almost palpable:

> Down the glimmering staircase, past the pensive clock,
> Childhood creeps on tiptoe, fumbles at the lock.
> Out of night escaping, toward the arch of dawn,
> What can childhood look for, over the wet lawn?

The documentary quality of his prose and poetry captures the essence of Weirleigh - the house, the garden and the distant prospect of the countryside: 'Looked at from our lawn, the Weald was, in my opinion, as good a view as anyone could wish to live with. You could run your eyes along more than twenty miles of low-hilled horizon never more than ten or twenty miles away. The farthest distance had the advantage of being near enough for its details to be, as it were, within recognisable reach. There was, for instance, a small party of pine trees on the skyline towards Maidstone which seemed to be keeping watch on the world beyond - a landmark on the limit of my experience they always seemed, those sentinel pines.'

John Stuart Forbes, Siegfried Sassoon, *Richard Cohen Books, 1999*

Cobtree Manor Zoo Park

Sir Garrard Tyrwhitt-Drake, best known as Mayor and generous benefactor of Maidstone, opened a Zoo Park in the 1930s at his Cobtree estate, just outside the town. Although the zoo has long since disappeared, Sir Garrard donated his estate to the town and it is now home to the Museum of Kent Life, a municipal golf-course and popular Country Park. A consummate showman, he describes here how the project started.

Once a traveller, always a traveller is in the main a very true saying, but when one has travelled a collection of wild animals from Maidstone to Scotland, Southend, Wembley, Sydenham, Margate, to say nothing of moving part of them every day from one town to another half-way over England and Scotland for thirty-four weeks, the time does come, even if it does not last permanently, when one says to oneself: "I think we will settle down for a bit, please." It was during the summer of 1933 that I decided that I had finished with travelling for a time. I had a large collection of animals, too big to keep as a hobby for myself alone, and I was naturally loath to part with any as most of them were old friends. I decided, therefore, that I would open my "zoo" to the public at Cobtree Manor, which is about two miles from the centre of Maidstone.

In 1910, in aid of the funds of the hospitals, they had proved quite popular and that, too, was before the days of mass motoring. I decided that I would open a Zoo Park round my home, and if the public liked it and patronized it, I would keep the whole of my collection intact, and if the public did not care for it and kept away, then I would have to reduce the inmates by seventy-five per cent and keep the remaining twenty-five percent for my own edification.

A collection of wild animals is not a cheap thing to run. Labour, food, insurances - for the animals against death and for the keepers and the public who may get damaged by the said insured animals - constant new, and repairs to old, cages, frequent replacement of inmates who die and get damaged, are a few of the items ever recurring.

My contract with the Crystal Palace finished in October and I at once hired the necessary transport to bring the whole lot, lock, stock, and barrel, to Maidstone.

It was no small caravan that trundled and lumbered home. Sixteen large cages each up to twenty feet long full of the larger animals, travelling boxes for the smaller fry, cage fronts, partitions, utensils of all sorts etc., filled the bodies of lorries that towed the big cages, and in due course the whole cavalcade arrived.

I was in my own mind very dubious if my venture would appeal to the public. I am afraid as a showman I am rather inclined to be a pessimist, and because of my doubts I did not want to spend money on permanent cages and buildings before I saw which way "the cat was likely to jump",

I had plenty of land for my Zoo Park and only had to decide how much of it I would utilize. I decided that I would start with ten acres of paddocks and orchard with space for parking some 400 cars - a number in my wildest dreams I never anticipated would pay me a visit on any one day; if possibly during a whole week!

Kent is the home of the hop and the Spanish chestnut woods. The former must climb, the latter supplies the poles up which they can do so. A Zoo Park must have hundreds of yards of wire netting fencing for birds, deer, wild sheep, etc., etc. I therefore purchased dozens of rolls of netting and hundreds of chestnut hop poles on which to attach it, and in a very short time I had paddocks for deer, emus, foreign sheep and geese.

Paths to anyone who has had to make and pay for them can be very expensive. With my doubts still strong as to my success I was anxious to be circumspect and economical! I therefore hit upon a scheme which made them good enough to suit the public and cheap enough to suit me, and I commend it to anyone who is in the same position as I was. Most of the paths were across fields, and all I did was to cut and remove the turf to the necessary width of the finished path; against the edge of the remaining turf I placed four by one-inch thick rough boards nailed to pegs driven into the ground, and then filled up between the boards on the ground from which the turf had been removed with fine ashes about three inches deep. A light roll and a rake levelled it down and the public trod it down hard.

Later, when I had decided that the zoo was a success and likely to be permanent, I gave the paths a good coat of tar, sprinkled it with three-quarter inch sharp ballast, and the result is an excellent hard wearing path, only requiring a fresh coating of tar and shingle occasionally, depending on the number of people who pass over it.

For the dangerous animals I used my travelling beast wagons drawn up in line on a concrete road I had prepared for them, their wheels covered by a wooden flap camouflaged to look like an old stone wall. An open monkey house, a range of cages for small animals, such as jackals, etc., a few aviaries, a large army hut for a café, a pay box and a kiosk completed the show.

On Monday, 26th March, 1934, the late Bertram Mills, like the good friend he was, came down to open it officially, supported, as the press described it, by a representative gathering of the county and the town, including practically every mayor and mayoress in Kent who were good enough to come and support their brother mayor of Maidstone - who was me!

When I look back on that opening I don't know how I had the cheek to present it; however, I did and my guests seemed quite pleased.

I had banked on paying my way if 40,000 visitors came in the season, and I even hoped that I might get 50,000 to 60,000.

The Monday after the opening was Easter Monday, and I was flooded out. I hoped for 3000 visitors, I got over 8000. I did my best and they were good tempered, but inside was chaotic, and the catering was swamped; still, the public was kind and pleased.

At the end of my first season (thirty-two weeks) 85,000 visitors had paid for admission and my wildest hopes of success had been far exceeded.

I was not such a fool as not to realize that the first year's attendance was hardly a reliable one on which to base calculations for the future, but I was satisfied that the people of Kent liked a Zoo Park and that I need not dispose of seventy-five per cent of my wild animals.

I should make it quite clear that my zoo is my hobby and not my livelihood, but I believe in conducting one's hobbies on business lines, and then if there is profit it can be put back into the hobby to improve it.

Acting on this I made several additions and improvements during the winter of 1934-5, including a small mammal house, a parrot house and laid out part of a wood as a wolf wood.

The next (and second) season, always a difficult one and much more a criterion of future years, gave me an attendance of 75,000 - a drop of 10,000 with considerably increased expenditure and a loss of some hundreds of pounds. Still, people spoke well of it and I looked forward to better times to come, and in the second winter added fox, dingo, pheasant and turkey enclosures in the wood.

The third season gave me an attendance of 100,000, and I then added a small aquarium and an elephant house with two young elephants, christened "Gert" and "Daisy" by my friends those inimitable artistes, the Waters sisters.

There is rather a funny story attached to the acquiring of those elephants and the house I prepared for them. The manager of Messrs Steel Brothers in Rangoon most kindly, through the good offices of a sub-manager who is a Maidstone man, offered to get me two female elephants. I said I wanted young, small ones, meaning three or four years old, standing four feet to four feet three inches at the shoulder. I was anxious that they should be shipped in crates because I foresaw the difficulty that might easily and probably would occur in getting them from the boat into a lorry this end for the last part of their journey. The sender was equally against crating them, and eventually the matter was compromised by the elephants being shipped on deck loose with the crates in sections in the hold.

It must be borne in mind I had never seen these animals. I did not know their age or their height.

In due course, having been advised of the time of the arrival of the boat at Tilbury, I hired a three-ton motor lorry with high body and went to collect them. Imagine my astonishment when I went on board to find that my baby elephants were two beasts five feet six inches high at the shoulder, weighing at least thirty hundredweight each.

The particular dock where the boat was berthed was an outer one connected with the main docks by a bridge over which a train goes but no motor lorry may. I dare not try and walk them from the quay to the lorry as I was afraid they might get in a panic and fall into the water, added to which if I got them to the lorry how in the world was I going to get them into it? I thanked my lucky stars I had insisted on those crates. There was nothing to be done but for the ship's carpenter, my men and everyone else we could get, to help put one of them together. Into this we pushed and pulled the two beasts and a crane lifted them out of the ship on to a railway truck, from which they were in due course lifted on to the motor lorry. The body we had had to strip to take the crate, for it overlapped each sides of the chassis in rather an alarming way, and the springs looked uncomfortably flat.

In due course they arrived safely in a house prepared for them. Here again it was a tight fit as far as the depth was concerned, and I am having to build a new one.

Last year, the fourth season, gave an attendance of 115,000, and I hope that the fifth, which finished on 30th October, 1938, will get within a reasonable distance of 150,000 which would be an increase of 100 per cent on the second season.

I have always been a great believer in the nimble tanner (6d) and would prefer to have 10,000 visitors at an admission fee of 6d than 5,500 at 1s. This may sound odd, but what I mean is 10,000 visitors satisfied are better than 5,500.

The finest advertisement one can have is one person telling his friends "such a good show, old man, and so very reasonable".

It is all right to advertise an attraction in the first case and to remind patrons thereafter, but if the article you advertise is not worth the money paid for it most certainly the public will not continue to want it.

The public of today has its peculiarities. It must keep having something fresh dished up for it. There must be something different. The same animals in different surroundings are just as good as new animals in old cages. At the same time many of the public visit the same zoo many times in a season, and not only know the animals but make friends with many of them and promptly miss one should it die or be disposed of.

People are always saying to me, "But how terribly interesting it must be to have a zoo of your own." Interesting is true, but there are a lot more adjectives which should be added to give a really true description! There is nothing I can conceive more worrying, nowhere where the unexpected happens at the most unexpected time and place, and nothing that keeps you so tied to it.

Sir Garrard Tywhitt-Drake, My Life with Animals, *Blackie, 1939*

In Lydd churchyard

Lieut. Thomas Edgar of Royal Navy who died October 17th, 1801
Aged 56. He came into the Navy at ten years of age, was in that
memorable engagement with Admiral Hawk, and sailed round the
world with the unfortunate Captain Cook of the "Resolution" in his
last voyage when he was killed by Indians at the Island of Owhie in
the South Seas 1778.

> Tom Edgar at last has sailed out of this world
> His shroud is put on and his topsails are furled,
> He lies snug in death's boat without any concern
> And is moored for a full due a'head and a'stern.
> Oe'r the Compass of life he has merrily run
> His voyage is completed his reckoning done.

Joe Grimaldi's Stuffed Cat

GRIMALDI'S GRIMAL-KIN - Among the many unique curiosities which
grace the bar of Mr Plaisted, wine and spirit merchant, in High Street,
Woolwich, is the stuffed remains of the celebrated Joey Grimaldi's
Cat. Puss was 27 years of age when she died, and had been in her
master's possession during the whole of that period, and till he died.
The remains of the well-known cock, which Joey used so
indescribably to introduce from his breeches pocket, and would
immediately flap his wings and crow in first-rate style, is also in the
possession of an individual in Woolwich, where this prince of mimics
passed the greater portion of his latter days.

Newspaper Cutting, 1838

11 · LEGENDS

Local News in Brenchley

Some 60 years ago, when I was a boy, it was the custom at Brenchley Church for the Clerk to hasten out before the Congregation left, and, taking up a position just outside the Church, call the attention of the people coming out by crying aloud, "O, yes! O, yes! O, yes!" He would then proceed to give notice of any news that might require circulating in the parish, such notices being of the most miscellaneous character; for example "Mr - has lost a pig;" or, "Mr - has a cow come astray;" and I have heard him give out that Mr - would kill a bull, on such a day, and sell it at so much a pound. This curious practice was resorted to because the parish roads were so bad that in wet weather they were almost impassable, and the parishioners rarely met, except on Sunday.

Joseph Stevens, The Kentish Notebook, *June 14th 1890*

The Bromley Pancake Bell

The curious custom of ringing the Pancake Bell on Shrove Tuesday is still observed at Bromley Church, although the reason for it is probably well-nigh forgotten. A tradition affirms that the ringer of the bell was supposed to be entitled to received one pancake from each house in the town. The original purpose of ringing the bell was to call the parishioners to the church, where the priest sat in an open chair, or stall, to hear the confessions of his people, to award them such penance as he thought good for them, or to give them absolution. The week preceding Lent was an appropriate time for all to perform that duty. It was for that reason called Shrove-tide, and the Tuesday in it was formerly and still is known as Shrove, Shrive or Confession Tuesday. On Shrove Tuesday, we are told by a writer in Notes and Queries, the housewives, in order to use up all the grease, lard, dripping, etc., made pancakes, and the apprentices and others about the house were summoned to a meal by the ringing of a bell (probably by the ringing of the confession bell), which was for that reason denominated the Pancake Bell.

George Clinch, Antiquarian Jottings, *Turnbull and Spears, 1889*

Dressing up in Broadstairs

A very ancient custom prevails of men and boys being dressed up in various ways to amuse people at Christmas. It unfortunately happened this year that a man dressed in a bear skin met a young woman named Crow, the wife of John Crow, Broadstairs, and alarmed her so much that she was obliged to go to a friend's house to recover herself; and in returning home she met the same man again, which so dreadfully alarmed her that she died the next day. A Coroner's inquest was held on the occasion, and handbills circulated to prohibit such practices in future,

Mockett's Journal, *1828*

ACKNOWLEDGEMENTS

I am grateful to the following for allowing the inclusion of both prose and poetry which remains in copyright: Countryside Books for extracts from *East Kent within Living memory*, East Kent Federation of Women's Institutes and *West Kent within living memory*, West Kent Federation of Women's Institutes; Sheil Land Associates for Edgar Johnson's, *Charles Dickens, His tragedy and triumph*, Allen Lane, 1952, 1977; Bailey Brothers and Swinfen Ltd for Joan Kent's *Wood Smoke and Pigeon Pie*; S.B. Publications for *The Kentish Magazine, 1850* quoted in Alan Major's *Cherries in the Rise*; Cassell & Co. for T.A. Layton's *A Year at the Peacock*; Pennant Books for Derek Coombe's *The Bawleyman*; © Kenneth Clark *Another Part of the Wood*, John Murray 1974, reproduced by permission of the Estate of the late Lord Clark, care of Margaret Hanbury, Literary Agent, 27 Walcot Square, London SE11 4UN, all rights reserved; Geoffrey Bles for *The Housekeeping Book of Susanna Whatman*; The King's England Press (www.kingsengland.com) for Arthur Mee's *The King's England: Kent*; David Higham Associates for James Lees-Milne's *People and Places* published by John Murray; extracts reproduced by kind permission from *Church Life in Kent*, by A.J. Willis, published in 1975 by Phillimore & Co Ltd, Shopwyke Manor Barn, Chichester, West Sussex PO20 2BG; Cranbrook and District Local History Society for C.C.R. Pile's, *Cranbrook Broadcloths and the Clothiers*; Cambridge University Press for John Conrad's, *Joseph Conrad: Times Remembered*, 1981; Centre for Kentish Studies for *The Diary of Charles Powell*, U934 F8; reproduced by permission of Pollinger Limited and the Estate of H.E. Bates *The Blossoming World*, Michael Joseph, 1971; Headley Brothers Ltd for C.H. Bishop's *Folkestone - the history of a town*, 1973; Ernest Benn for Doris Langley Moore's *E. Nesbit*; Richard Cohen Books for John Stuart Forbes' *Siegfried Sassoon*; Blackie for Sir Garrard Tywhitt-Drake's *My Life with animals*; for the extract from *A Kentish Lad* by Frank Muir, published by Bantam Press, used by permission of Transworld Publishers, a division of The Random House Group Ltd; John Murray for John Betjeman's *Margate 1940* in his *Collected Poems* and Richard Cobb's *Something to Hold Onto*; H.G. Wells, *Kipps*, Everyman, 1993 reproduced by permission of A.P. Watt Ltd on behalf of The Literary Executors of the Estate of H.G. Wells; Berkshire Record Office for *A Tour into Kent*; *Hop-Picking* by George Orwell (Copyright © George Orwell, 1931) by permission of Bill Hamilton as the Literary Executor of the Estate of the Late Sonia Brownell Orwell and Secker & Warburg Ltd; HarperCollins Publishers Ltd © 1967, Harold Nicolson, *Diaries and Letters 1939-45*, edited by Nigel Nicolson.

The publishers have endeavoured to contact all holders of copyright, but will be pleased to correct any omissions or errors in future editions.